WHEN LOST MEN COME HOME

REVISED EDITION

*An Inspired Journey
to Sexual Integrity*

by

DAVID ZAILER

ENDORSEMENTS

When Lost Men Come Home is an inspiring read and study for any man or woman who wants to restore their sanity from the ravages of sexual addiction, and for those who want to make right their relationship with God — some for the first time. Through revealing personal glimpses into the author's own journey, David Zailer invites the reader to surrender their addiction for a life of integrity. Zailer is never heavy-handed, and those who have spent time on their own spiritual quest will want to walk along beside him and reexamine their own definition of a Higher Power. This book is a must-read for men and women who want to "come home" in their own spiritual quest and how it relates to their recovery from sexual addiction.

ALEXANDRA KATEHAKIS, PHD, CSAT-S, CST-S
FOUNDER AND CLINICAL DIRECTOR CENTER FOR HEALTHY SEX, LOS ANGELES, CA
www.thecenterforhealthysex.com

David Zailer goes beyond recovery to keys to revitalize your spiritual vitality. This book is a great plan to get your life back if it has been stolen by the cheap thrills of sexual and moral compromise.

STEPHEN ARTERBURN
AUTHOR, FOUNDER OF WOMEN OF FAITH, AND HOST OF *NEWLIFE LIVE!*
www.newlife.com

I have had the privilege of working with men and women with addictions for the past ten years. David Zailer's book *When Lost Men Come Home* has been the "go-to" book I recommend for sexual addiction. His warm, caring manner and his honest, humble heart towards those who struggle with sexual addiction create an environment for healing that emanates from deep within, where the struggle takes place. David uses the simplicity of the Twelve Steps along with his deeply personal relationship with Christ to lead lost men to a fulfilling life of peace, freedom, and joy.

Nina Dreyer, LCSW
Clinical Director of Encompass Recovery
www.theeffect.org

David Zailer weaves a tapestry of integrity and spirituality recounting his past struggles with alcohol, drugs, and sex addiction, and how faith led him to a life of meaningful serenity. He enhances our understanding of the magic of the Twelve Steps, and how their principles guided his journey, and the journey of his fellow travelers in recovery. *When Lost Men Come Home* gives sexually addicted men and women authentic hope and direction so they can be successful in their recovery journey.

Tina Wehner, MTSC, LCMHCS, CSAT-S, CHFP
Hope & Freedom Counseling Services
Cornelius NC 28031

When Lost Men Come Home by David Zailer provides a transparently honest narrative of the hopelessness of addiction and the hopefulness of recovery through Christ. I am convinced the Lord will use *Lost Men* to bring hope and direction to those who are still lost in their addiction.

Reverend Laird Bridgman, PsyD, C.E.A.P.
www.rsaministries.org

At our treatment center, we attempt to reach the whole man and his underlying issues that keep him trapped in his addictions to drugs and alcohol. Most of our male clients come to us with early-childhood sexual abuse issues or sexual addiction as a co-occurring disorder. We have found Dave's book to be insightful, practical, and effective, and we have adopted it as a valued component of our curriculum. *When Lost Men Come Home* gives men the hope that helps transform their compulsions into sobriety and their brokenness into lives of integrity.

Richard E. Jackson, CEO
Covenant Hills Treatment Centers
www.covenanthillstreatment.com

When I met David Zailer, I realized quickly that we shared much philosophical common ground at the clinical and spiritual levels. In our work as a recovery ministry, faith community, and treatment center, many of our clients have backstories that include sexual abuse and addiction, so it is comforting to know that David and Operation Integrity are there to help in these areas. Our clients have told us how much *When Lost Men Come Home* has helped them, and as one client in particular said, "Finally a book about my issues that I can really understand."

DAVE BRISBIN, MDIV, RASI
LEAD PASTOR, THEEFFECT
www.theeffect.org

When Lost Men Come Home is a practical approach to recovery through the Twelve Steps. David Zailer uses his own poignant journey to guide readers through a process that he aptly describes as both simple and hard. Those struggling with sex addiction will find help through David's guidance.

MILTON S. MAGNESS, DMIN, MPSY, CSAT
AUTHOR OF *HOPE & FREEDOM FOR SEXUAL ADDICTS AND THEIR PARTNERS* AND *THIRTY DAYS TO HOPE & FREEDOM FROM SEXUAL ADDICTION*
www.hopeandfreedom.com

This book, *When Lost Men Come Home,* speaks clearly into a difficult and frightening reality of human experience. David Zailer has a way of blending scriptural principles with the time-proven effectiveness of the Twelve Step recovery movement. He speaks from his own inspired journey, revealing important factual truth, and boldly sharing God's promise to transform lives. Read this book and then share it with someone else. It may save your life and someone else's too.

TERRY LaDOW, MS, BCPCC, CADCII
www.terryladow.com

When Lost Men Come Home (Third Edition) © 2023 by David Zailer
When Lost Men Come Home – Not for Men Only (Second Edition) © 2012 by David Zailer
When Lost Men Come Home (First Edition) © 2006 by David Zailer

Published by Homecoming Books for

OPERATION
INTEGRITY

Copyright © 2023 by David Zailer

Edited by Jessica Snell

Cover Design and Internal Setup by Kirsten Doukas, pastelblackdesign.com

Library of Congress Control Number: 2022918885

Paperback: 979-8-9870757-0-8
E-Book: 979-8-9870757-1-5

For those who know they need help.

TABLE OF CONTENTS

INTRODUCTION

Several years before I wrote the first edition of this book, I began making notes about my personal journey recovering from sexual addiction. I don't recall what first motivated me to put my thoughts on paper. The only thing I remember was that I had hope that the recovery experiences shared between me and others could possibly help more people.

A few months into this process, a church in my community suggested that I facilitate a porn addiction recovery group for men in our area. I wasn't interested at first, but someone pointed out there was no one better for the job. Few people have excelled in obsessive lustfulness like I have.

Our recovery group started with three men. Then we had four, then six, ten, fifteen, twenty — and the group continued to grow over the years. We came from all walks of life, and each of us had a sincere desire to change our lives. This group of men was the early nucleus of Operation Integrity. We were a mixed bag of nuts and a merry band of characters. I continued to write, but my writing took a new direction. I became more of a listener, and wrote more about what I heard than what I knew to write on my own. I was working to capture the thoughts and feelings of others. This work helped me capture my own thoughts and feelings.

Several years later, women joined us in the recovery process. They brought great depth and courage to our process. Individual meetings remained specifically for men or for women, but it was clearly evident that sexual addiction was not only "a man's issue."

At Operation Integrity, we recognize that a great number of men and women will struggle with their sexual integrity at some time in their lives. The hurtful impact can be staggering, crossing all social, ethnic, economic, and religious boundaries. The greatest problem is that most people do not know, will not accept, and cannot admit they have a struggle, let alone admit they have an addiction. Even if they did recognize and admit their need, where would they go for help?

Thankfully, we learned to admit our struggles and having done so, we have begun to overcome them. We also know what our bad decisions have cost us in terms of our relationships, our marriages, our children, our time, money, and energy. Thankfully, once again, we saw a way to change our lives. Through a Christ-centered application of the Twelve Step recovery process, we have experienced a transforming movement toward health and wholeness. Moreover, we have discovered a new, enthusiastic outlook for life. We found our individual and collective voices, with which we share an informed message of encouragement.

The following pages are the heard, observed, and expressed experiences of our shared recovery journey, as well as certain aspects of my recovery. No one stands above anyone else; our voices are a chorus. We are the sound of struggling but mighty men and women, sharing our lives personally and deeply, in forthright and transparent unison.

We don't own the song of freedom we sing. The song belongs to God. He sang it to us, and we sing it to you. We invite you to discover the freedom your heart longs to know, and to sing along.

ABOUT THE THIRD EDITION

When Lost Men Come Home was first published in 2006. Its sole purpose was to be a small, bound book to hold observations from the first Operation Integrity fellowship. It was a rough publication, but straightforward, with quality content derived from the shared group experience of our early fellowship. It proved to be of great value to many.

In 2012, the title was changed to *When Lost Men Come Home — Not For Men Only*. The content was updated to reflect the important wisdom that women brought to our understanding.

This third edition, *When Lost Men Come Home: An Inspired Journey to Sexual Integrity,* brings simplified writing and expresses more of the enduring hopefulness that comes from working a Twelve Step recovery program over time. It focuses on *the process* of recovery, and seeks to avoid the temptation of making a *product* for popularity or profit.

THE PROBLEM

Addiction is a medical and clinical term referring to physiological and psychological dependencies that exhibit themselves in destructive behavioral patterns.

In layman's terms, *addiction is a destructive relationship with any mood- or mind-altering substance or experience.* It is a complex human phenomenon manifesting in physical, psychological, sociological, and spiritual ways.

Addiction has been called the most human of all diseases. *No one is entirely immune.*

Sexual addiction might be the most misunderstood of all addictions. Simply stated, *sexual addiction is the loss of control over destructive sexual behavior or relationships.* Perhaps the most helpful definition is a practical one: *Habitual sexual behavior that harms one's life.*

A *sex addict* is someone who utilizes their sexual experiences to alter their mood or state of mind in a way that is destructive to them and their relationships. Most often thought of as inappropriate sexual behavior, sexual addiction can be present with no obvious inappropriate behavior. Even married monogamous people can be addicted sexually if they overly depend on "appropriate" sex to maintain their sense of well-being. Sex is obviously fundamental to human life, but when someone uses their sexuality as if it were a drug to medicate silent, haunting emotions that remain hidden deep inside, the healthy connection between their inner soul and their sexuality is eroded, and it becomes destructive.

Sexual addiction is not really about sex at all. It is about lost and broken intimacy.

To be alive is to be addicted, and to be alive and addicted is to stand in need of grace.

~ Gerald G. May, MD, *Addiction & Grace*

A SOLUTION

The vision of Operation Integrity is to help people recover from addiction, leading to radical life transformation. We start by offering basic education about addiction. We also encourage participation in a community that supports recovery. We encourage spiritual growth through a personal Twelve Step journey coupled with counseling or therapy. Finally, we endorse *spiritual formation* practices that lead to deepening intimacy with God.

- We propose these six disciplines be part of one's life:

- Be involved in a Twelve Step recovery fellowship that is specific to one's area of struggle.

- Meet with a qualified therapist or counselor.

- Work the Twelve Step process at a personal level, which includes the guidance of a sponsor and reading relevant recovery literature.

- Encourage family involvement through counseling, Al-Anon, Co-Dependents Anonymous, or similar Twelve Step support fellowships for spouses and loved ones.

- Address underlying causes and triggers. Underlying causes may be an obsessive need for affirmation, unhealed family of origin issues, childhood abuse or abandonment, unhealed grief, hidden feelings of inferiority or superiority, and/or an unhealthy view of God (which often exists most profoundly in people who have had significant religious training).

- Address other addictions like overeating, alcohol and other drugs, gambling, unhealthy relationships, obsessive religious activity, etc.

THE TWELVE STEPS

Adapted from Alcoholics Anonymous

STEP ONE   We admitted we were powerless over our addictions, that our lives had become unmanageable.

STEP TWO   We came to believe that a Power greater than ourselves could restore us to sanity.

STEP THREE   We made a decision to turn our will and our lives over to the care of God as we understood Him.

STEP FOUR   We made a searching and fearless moral inventory of ourselves.

STEP FIVE   We admitted to God, to ourselves, and to another human being the exact nature of our wrongs.

STEP SIX   We became entirely ready to have God remove all these defects of character.

STEP SEVEN   We humbly asked Him to remove our shortcomings.

STEP EIGHT   We made a list of all persons we had harmed, and became willing to make amends to them all.

STEP NINE   We made direct amends to such people wherever possible, except when to do so would injure them or others.

Step Ten   We continued to take personal inventory and when we were wrong, promptly admitted it.

Step Eleven   Sought through prayer and meditation to improve our conscious contact with God as we understood Him, praying only for the knowl edge of His will for us and the power to carry that out.

Step Twelve   Having had a spiritual awakening as the result of these Steps, we tried to carry the message to others, and to practice these principles in all our affairs.

SERENITY PRAYER

Attributed to Reinhold Niebuhr

God grant me the Serenity to accept the things I cannot change; Courage to change the things I can; and the Wisdom to know the difference. Living one day at a time; accepting hardship as a pathway to peace; taking, as Jesus did, this sinful world as it is, not as I would have it: Trusting that You will make all things right if I surrender to Your will; that I may be reasonably happy in this life and supremely happy with You forever in the next.

Amen

OPERATION INTEGRITY PRAYER

God, I pray that I will learn to desire obedience more than blessing or comfort and to know that the greatest blessing in life is to live obedient to Your will. May I learn to better give up my will and find my complete and total satisfaction in Your will. My self-centeredness destroys me but seeking You and doing Your will brings life to me. Realizing this, I have decided that my mind, my heart, and my will, will be directed to You. I will find my purpose and identity in knowing You more personally and living more powerfully according to Your Spirit.

Amen

THE AUTHOR'S STORY

As a teenager and young adult, I thought very little about my childhood. But in the early years of my recovery I began to think back about my life growing up. I remembered my mother battled mental illness, a battle that she eventually lost to suicide. My father was a much-loved church musician. He also had a secret stash of pornography. As a young boy, I looked at it whenever I could get away with it. When I was eight, a family friend from church took an interest in me. He took me fishing and to baseball games, and he molested me.

Consistent with my family's pattern of secret keeping, I never told anyone.

I'm not sure which was more damaging: being molested or knowing how my father cheated on my mother through his use of pornography.

By age nine, I began to have behavioral problems. The molestation continued and I continued to keep it secret. I was flunking school, barred from some after-school activities, and was too disruptive for many Sunday School teachers. I was finally examined by a child psychiatrist and diagnosed as mentally retarded. The doctors prescribed medication to control my behavior, and I was placed in a special class at school for mentally disadvantaged children.

My name became "retard."

People at church said that God loved all the little children — yellow, brown, black, and white. I felt invisible and overlooked. I thought I must be different than the other children. Perhaps I was some strange, ugly color in comparison to them. Did God ever take time to notice me? Would he even care about me if he did?

I became defensive and competitive, determined to prove my value. As an adolescent, I would sit alone in my bedroom reading *The Living Bible,* praying, and pleading that God would make me useful and worthwhile.

I heard only silence in return.

By my early twenties, I had lost hope of ever having a happy life, and I began to drink alcohol. It started innocently: my first beer was with friends from church as we shared a pizza. I hated the taste of the beer but loved the warm feeling, the self-confidence, and the perceived freedom the alcohol gave me. It was a magical answer of sorts. Within two weeks of that first beer, I was drinking as often as I could. Years went by, and I began to work weekends in a bar, where I discovered cocaine and other drugs. Over the next few years, several acquaintances of mine were murdered and I saw many lives destroyed.

In 1989, I moved to the West Coast to start a new life. I started a business, made it successful, and began attending church once again. I smiled and pretended life was great, but deep inside I couldn't escape feelings of self-hatred, and the thought that everyone would be better off if I was gone. After a few years of abstaining from drugs and alcohol by willpower alone, I periodically began to drink again, and soon the drugs followed. Where I had previously been a cocaine user of generally small amounts, I became a binge user of larger amounts, and added crystal meth and heroin to the drugs I used.

In 1999, I went on my last drug binge. I had planned a little weekend getaway, but I ended up traveling around Southern California for three weeks, smoking $500 worth of crack cocaine every day, rarely eating or sleeping. I overdosed three times and was arrested on drug charges three times. After each arrest, I bailed myself out of jail to head back on the road for more.

I thought I was having fun.

A few days later, while sitting in a seedy hotel room, I called a friend that I had met at the church I was attending. Bob M. was a recovering alcoholic who attended AA meetings. For several months, I had confided in him about my drug use and my sense of hopelessness. He was the one person I knew who seemed to understand the anguish I felt, so I trusted him. Bob convinced me to stop drinking and taking drugs and to get some rest. Later that night, he drove several hours to pick me up and bring me home.

Once I was home, I had to face the consequences. The authorities wanted me to serve time in prison; it seemed I had finally destroyed my life. However, following my attorney's recommendation, I entered a drug and alcohol treatment program that combined counseling and the Twelve Steps. This program educated me about the reality of my addictions and gently addressed the self-destructive thoughts that lay hidden behind everything I did. The early months in that program prepared me for the most important day of my life.

That day began with my attorney calling me in the morning to say that things were not looking good for me with the prosecutor and court, and that I should prepare to serve time in prison. That same day, in the afternoon, my counselor at the treatment program asked me to tell him about my belief in God. I told him everything I knew about God from church and Sunday School. He listened for a while as I droned on about the facts of Christian history, but then, with obvious frustration, he told me that he didn't want to hear any more. I was shocked, and asked him why. His response was simple and direct. "David, I think you need to find a real Jesus. I think you need to find a real God."

His words angered me. With a bit of a snarl, I asked him why he would say such a terrible thing. Once again, his words were simple and direct but also gentle. "Well, David, it's obvious that the God and the Jesus that you say you believe in haven't done you much good, have they?"

The words he spoke pierced my heart like an arrow! I sat stunned as his question sunk in. It made me face the reality of how my religious professions had left me morally and spiritually bankrupt — void of the necessary power to successfully live life.

My religious belief deflated like a broken balloon.

I had a meeting with my friend Bob that night to talk over what I needed to do to prepare for prison. I waited for him in an empty parking lot. It was dark and wet, cold and windy. As I stood there shivering, I looked up at the stars and pondered my life.

I was $100,000 in debt. My family would not speak to me. My friends were tired of me. My business associates barely tolerated me. I had overdosed several times and had come close to being killed a few times. I was in drug rehab, and worst of all by far, all I really wanted that cold, dark, agonizing night was more alcohol and cocaine.

Crushed by the weight of it all, I looked up and said, "Oh God! I am a drug addict and I need your help, but I don't even know who you are. I am willing to call you any name you want me to, but if you don't help me, I'm afraid I'm going to die."

At that moment, and for the first time in my life, I found the beginning of personal honesty and accepted myself for who I was — a child in need. Everything was unimportant except for one thing — either God would help me, or I was as good as dead.

God was no longer a *religious* belief; God was a life-or-death issue.

Standing there alone, with nothing but my desperate prayer, I heard a voice respond, "Alright, David, now I can go to work."

Startled, I whirled around, looking for who had spoken, but there was no one there. I looked behind the bushes next to the building. I looked under the cars in the parking lot. I lifted the lid of the trash dumpster to look inside. I looked everywhere but saw no one.

I wondered if I might be going crazy, but I also sensed something big had happened. I sensed my prayer had been heard and felt like things might possibly be different in the future. I sensed that the battle for my life had been joined with power adequate to change what most needed to be changed — me! For the first time I could remember, I knew I didn't have to be alone, and I had a genuine desire to live.

Ultimately, the court showed mercy by giving me the opportunity of long-term rehabilitation instead of prison. Today, motivated by a spiritual power deep within me, I continue following the God who showed up to save me, and he continues to do the work that only he can do — changing me from the inside out.

I have discovered beautiful gifts such as mercy, hope, courage, and a gentle love for myself and others. These gifts enable me to do things I never dreamed of doing. I was even baptized while attending a Christian men's retreat, where I learned that people had been praying for me for several years before my arrest.

Now, decades later, I am still receiving new and beautiful gifts. My favorite one is gratitude for life. My childhood misfortune and my addictions to alcohol, drugs, and sex have become a valuable part of what I believe to be a well-scripted plan for my life. With the simple surrender of my will and life, I continue discovering God in a loving, personal way.

I have come to understand that my life story actually has little to do with me. It has everything to do with God, and much to do with you. Passion compels me to tell others about the one who gives mercy and grace to addicted sinners like me. If he gives mercy and grace to me, he will certainly give it to you, and to anyone who asks.

> *Praise be to the God and Father of our Lord Jesus Christ, the Father of compassion and the God of all comfort, who comforts us in all our troubles, so that we can comfort those in any trouble with the comfort we ourselves receive from God.*
>
> *~ 2 CORINTHIANS 1:3–4*

THE END — THE BEGINNING

We admitted we were powerless over our addictions, that our lives had become unmanageable.

~ STEP ONE FROM THE TWELVE STEPS

And I know that nothing good lives in me, that is, in my sinful nature. I want to do what is right, but I can't.

~ ROMANS 7:18 NLT

I am worn out from sobbing. All night I flood my bed with weeping, drenching it with my tears. My vision is blurred by grief; my eyes are worn out because of all my enemies. Go away, all you who do evil, for the LORD has heard my weeping. The LORD has heard my plea; the LORD will answer my prayer.

~ PSALM 6:6–9 NLT

I am exhausted and completely crushed. My groans come from an anguished heart. You know what I long for, Lord; you hear my every sigh. My heart beats wildly, my strength fails, and I am going blind.

~ PSALM 38:8–10 NLT

I never wanted to become a sex addict. As a matter of fact, getting addicted to anything was the furthest thing from my mind. Nevertheless, various sorts of addictions grew inside of me over time and almost destroyed me.

The recovery process has helped me understand the roots of my addictions; I believe it started when I was eight years old. Abuses that I experienced as a child, and my family history of addiction, increased the likelihood of addiction in me as an adult. I could point fingers, but blaming others doesn't do any good. Learning what lies beneath addiction is what is helpful. Learning to live free from self-destructiveness is what is most important if I want to have a healthy and happy future.

EMPOWERED IN POWERLESSNESS

On most days, I realize how powerless I am — in my own power, that is — to find the freedom my soul longs to know. Having said this, I also experience joyous freedom each day because I stopped engaging old self-destructive habits.

Healthy living helps us enjoy life to the fullest.

However, there are some days when I feel I might catapult myself into a darkness that far exceeds my own ability to escape. I will never forget how sexual addiction brings a conflict of mind, spirit, and body, brutalizing me at the core of who I am.

Can you relate?

Those who have struggled with repeated patterns of sexually destructive behavior, and who are honest with themselves, understand this powerlessness — but we often have trouble admitting it. Recognizing and admitting personal powerlessness is a fundamental principle that must be accepted before any of us will find life-giving recovery.

Just like alcoholics in recovery, healing begins once we honestly admit we have a problem.

I almost died in depression and shame before I accepted this simple truth. But once I got honest about the feeble and powerless aspect of my life, I saw how I had been trapped in a long, downward spiral. Ego-centered self-confidence had kept me in the grip of my addictions. I know of many others who continue to claim confidence in themselves alone, even after countless failures. Their obsession with self-confidence kills them a little more every day.

STRENGTH IN NUMBERS

Everyone who participates in Operation Integrity has their own story to tell, but we are united together as one fellowship. We are a community of survivors who intuitively understand each other's experiences. Yes, our experiences are different, with unique behavioral patterns and consequences. But nevertheless, we see ourselves reflected in one another and we focus on what we share in common. This is how we benefit individually from the strength the fellowship offers to us as a whole. But it is also more than that: along with the good, we also share one another's sufferings and shortcomings.

RECOVERY IS BOTH HARD AND SIMPLE

Addiction recovery work is not fashionable or exclusive. It is gritty work, with lots of twists and turns. We might even run off the road into a ditch on occasion. But even though the work is hard, it is also simple. All that is required is sincere openness of mind, the courage to be honest, and willingness to do the work. Honest spiritual growth is the overarching, essential ingredient needed to recover from sexual addiction.

Through the power of spiritual renewal, our addictions heal with amazing simplicity.

Trying Harder Can Make Things Worse

Let me offer a thoughtful caveat here: spiritual growth doesn't often happen the way we expect it to. I grew up attending a large denominational church, and many in our fellowship maintained long, dedicated commitments to their church family. But others of us came from no particular religious belief system at all. Some of us even considered ourselves agnostic or atheist when we joined our fellowship.

Regardless of the religion I professed, I was functionally an atheist because my addictions increased no matter what I claimed to believe. I had made repeated commitments to stop, but I had lost touch with reality as I professed recommitments to God and to religious practice. Even though I was sincere in my attempts, I tried and failed more times than I could count. No amount of self-determination, self-asserted effort, or religious activity protected me from the compulsions that came with my addictions. I found no effective plan, method, or power to overcome my addictions, or the shame that always followed them. The harder I tried to beat my addictions, the worse they got.

How Addiction Starts

Addictions begin in subtle and seemingly benign patterns of destructive behavior that are easy to ignore at first. The destructiveness of sexual addiction comes from internal dynamics such as shame, embarrassment, loneliness, emotional isolation, and exhaustion — an endless stream of painful feelings that any one of us can experience. *Any pattern of emotional mismanagement and pleasurable, but unhealthy, behavior can feed the growth of addiction.* Before someone even thinks to question if they are sexually addicted, the addiction may already be deeply rooted inside of them.

In my case, I tried to make "good" use of my addicted inclinations. They entertained me when I was bored. Comforted me when I was hurting. Distracted me from painful childhood memories and my failures as a young adult. I considered them harmless pleasures and didn't suffer obvious negative consequences at first. But deep within my heart, I hated what I was doing. I worked hard to stop my destructive behaviors, often slowing down or even stopping for periods of time. Yet all the while, addiction continued to grow inside of me, silently gaining control.

Our loneliest places inside are the fertile ground where sexual addiction can take hold. These are places so deep, we cannot reach or heal them by ourselves.

Our hidden beliefs, our unconscious thinking, our unrecognized feelings, are at the deep center of our addictions. With ineffective care and life management, anyone can become frustrated, fearful, dissocialized, and resentful. This is why we often reach for something that makes us feel good — and sex can make you feel very good indeed.

At least for a moment or two.

HOPELESSNESS RULED

Once I had lost the ability to permanently stop my addictive behaviors, the only life I knew was one of hopelessness, fear, and shame. I had tried everything, but nothing had worked for me. I hated my behavior, but most of all, I had come to hate myself. Destruction grew inside of me and consequence grew around me. Though I wanted to with all my heart, I could not stop the accelerating madness that had overtaken me. There were times, however, when I thought I was in control and that everything would be okay. But I was only deceiving myself, suffering the hard bedrock of addiction: denial.

Denial uses plausible-sounding but illogical reasoning to blind us to the destructive reality of our lives. In plain terms: *when I am in the grip of denial,* I **D**on't **E**ven k**N**ow **I A**m **L**ying.

In fellowship at Operation Integrity, we talk about how we could sometimes bridle and contain ourselves for extended periods of time, only to see our addicted compulsions ooze into other areas of our lives. A man who had visited massage parlors would stop visiting them for a while and believe he had conquered his problem. Or a woman addicted to romance novels and pornography stopped using them, and was convinced that she had conquered her dirty little secrets.

Success!, they thought. They were feeling great!

But sooner rather than later, they found themselves behaving addictively in other areas of their lives: with alcohol, drugs, prescription medications, food, spending, gambling, work, or even an obsessive preoccupation with controlling other people.

The list of addictions is almost endless. The results are similarly destructive.

Most of us substituted or rotated our addictions in one way or another. Our best efforts to gain control had changed little except the tones and textures of our destructive patterns. This showed how we suffered from dark secrets, toxic shame, and a laundry list of inner struggles. We were masters of ignoring our addicted reality. Denial was a dominant power in our lives.

In rare moments of clarity, we would glimpse the insane thinking behind our rationalizations, our minimizations, and our excuses. But a moment later, we would forget the pain our addictive behavior caused. We would believe that all was well, that we were in control, that we could eat our cake and have it too. No matter how often we had hurt ourselves and others, we held on to the same old efforts in hope they would bring a better result in the future.

This actually makes sense if you don't know a better way to manage your pain. It is also delusional thinking which opens the door to more addictive behavior. Soon we were acting out once again, always with the same result. Insanity!

(Definition of insanity: *Doing the same thing over and over again while expecting different results.*)

Here is an important point to consider: any addiction that is not acknowledged and surrendered will most likely intensify in obsessiveness, frequency, and negative consequence. Unhealed addictions almost always progress, although the addicted person usually doesn't see it. Addictions outsmart people in this way. An immensely complex human phenomenon, addiction is fluid, odorless, and colorless in all its forms. The pioneers of addiction recovery, Alcoholics Anonymous, assert that addictions are "cunning, baffling and powerful."

I found my own addictions to be incredibly patient. They hid inside of me, waiting to strike at the most destructive moment. Without fail, whenever I acted out in my addiction, my inner life and my outer circumstances would erode, and my relationships would suffer. Inch by inch, addiction eroded my dignity and my humanity. I felt dead inside, and spiritually I was. My addictions cost me the most precious of God-given human dignities: the clear ability to make healthy and sane choices for myself.

Evil wins when we chase after instant gratification.

Victims of Our Choices

Many in our fellowship admitted how they felt victimized by those around them. More often than not, they were really victimizing themselves. We had fought harder and harder to hang on to the life we thought we wanted, and yet each day we had lost a little more of that life because of our self-destructive behavior. Of course this increased our guilt and shame, which led to even more destructive acting out. Sexual addiction had corrupted the values and principles we professed. We did what the addiction demanded instead of what we truly wanted to do. In one way or another, everything we said had become a lie. No one believed us but us. All that we could honestly say was that *we wanted to want to stop.*

In the years before I recognized my addicted condition, I had known others who suffered from obviously apparent addictions. I couldn't relate to them because of my denial.

I would say things like, "Poor guy, too bad he never got his act together."

Or, "Thank God I'm not like him. I can stop whenever I want."

Or perhaps, "I'm not like him; I'm only having a good time."

Many times, I said, "I'm not hurting anyone if no one finds out."

Have you had similar thoughts about others, or yourself?

Denial is a common struggle. It keeps us from recognizing the common ground we share with the addicted people we publicly like to pity, and secretly like to condemn.

One might think that sexual addiction was my biggest problem, but it wasn't. My biggest problem was my denial and my addiction to my self-sufficiency — the delusional belief that I was in control. Little did I know, denial was a major force behind every addictive thought I had and every destructive action I took. AA calls this "self-will run riot; natural instincts gone awry."

Our God-given instincts turn against us when we live as if we are the masters of our own world. An attitude like this causes us to lose sight of our true needs and desires. It is self-inflicted blindness, and will lead us to places we do not want to go.

Because of my denial, my life had been dominated by a warped sense of what I needed and wanted, and not what was good for me. Even more, my obsession to control myself, my circumstances, and the lives of others was more hurtful than I could have imagined. I rationalized my actions to myself because I couldn't explain my actions. I made excuses to others because I didn't have reasonable answers to their questions. I was obsessed with looking normal, so I hid my need for help so that no one would suspect the false image I worked so hard to present. Then, unable to tolerate my inauthenticity and false bravado, I would long for the emotional relief my addictions could bring, and I would return to what had poisoned me time and time again.

"Hell on Earth" is where the men and women of our fellowship have lived. The way to freedom appeared when we admitted that our self-centeredness was too much for us to handle by ourselves. We admitted how our isolation and secrets had made us ever more frantic, even as we looked for ever more grandiose ways to prove ourselves worthy to people around us.

We admitted we had been fools and had not known it!

Without help, will a fool ever know?

THE CRUSH OF SHAME

Shame brings misguided rules and regulations to control and condemn us, with ever harsher penalties when we fail. Shame builds a world of hiding and lies, with brutal consequences when we are found out and exposed. Shame is a deep sense of personal condemnation. Shame makes us wonder if God regrets creating us. Shame makes us wonder if everyone else would be happier if we just went away. Shame erodes our physical, emotional, and spiritual health. Shame makes us feel mentally, emotionally, and spiritually sick. Shame drives us away from people, so we feel increasingly isolated and lonely, and we stay stuck in self-loathing. As we become lost in shame, we become our own harshest judge and addiction becomes our personalized form of self-execution.

Our loved ones did their best to make up the distance between us, but shame made us run from real intimacy. We often rewarded their love with broken promises to clean up our act, so many of them eventually lost hope. Feeling all the more abandoned and hurt, we agreed with their hurt and angry view of us. We grew to be resentful, which of course drove us even further away from our loved ones. Sometimes our friends and families cut ties with us for their own emotional well-being. Who could blame them?

We wondered where God was, and we had questions we were afraid to ask.

Why are people abandoning me?

Why doesn't God solve my problems?

Why doesn't God straighten me up?

In denial and shame, we had become archenemies to our own well-being, and lost in an imaginary war with God. We were alone, desperate, and dying, and blind to the insanity of it all.

Perhaps scripture says it best:

I live in disgrace all day long, and my face is covered with shame at the taunts of those who reproach and revile me, because of the enemy, who is bent on revenge.

~ *PSALM 44:15–16*

GIVING UP THE FIGHT

In the midst of the beatings I had inflicted upon myself, I gave up the fight to control my addictions. With a demoralized, ego-crushing sadness, I surrendered my need to be stronger than I really was. I admitted first to myself, and then to others, that I was powerless over my sexual addiction and that my life was beyond my ability to manage on my own. In that moment of anguish, I had a lifesaving encounter with truth. My ego had been broken for the better. There was only one choice: to live or to die.

By admitting that I was powerless over my addiction, and acknowledging my failure to manage my life, I had made a life-saving decision — a miracle in itself, really — a claim for personal honesty. This decision was the first investment necessary to save my life. It was an investment that only I could make.

"It's the way you've lived that's brought all this on you. The bitter taste is from your evil life. That's what's piercing your heart."

~ *JEREMIAH 4:18 MSG*

Those who are honest and fortunate will find themselves standing at this painful crossroad, and they will know that they can no longer hide from the inevitable question.

What will it be: Your sexual addiction, or your surrender leading to a new life?

Isn't this an ever-important question for all of us?

The decision to surrender my stubborn independence brought a new perspective that enabled me to see what I couldn't see before. Though I didn't fully realize it at the time, I had begun *the process* of becoming a healthy, whole person. I had hit bottom, or perhaps, I had chosen to hit bottom.

Humiliation had become a springboard toward humility.

My "wanting to want to stop" began to make sense. The truth was clear to see; I do not have, and will never have, the dubious and sick luxury of self-deception!

A better future waits for us at rock bottom.

PERSONAL REFLECTIONS

PERSONAL REFLECTIONS

FINDING REAL HOPE

We came to believe that a Power greater than ourselves could restore us to sanity.

~ STEP TWO FROM THE TWELVE STEPS

"Everything is possible for one who believes."

~ MARK 9:23

"Don't panic. I'm with you. There's no need to fear for I'm your God. I'll give you strength. I'll help you. I'll hold you steady, keep a firm grip on you."

~ ISAIAH 41:10 MSG

You can be sure that God will take care of everything you need, his generosity exceeding even yours in the glory that pours from Jesus.

~ PHILIPPIANS 4:19 MSG

Throughout all my teen and young adult years of church attendance and religious profession, I struggled and failed to permanently stop using pornography. My use of porn triggered cravings for alcohol and other drugs. In addition to alcohol, I used cocaine and heroin, and I dabbled in methamphetamine. As is often the case with those who use drugs, I was arrested for drug possession. Instead of jail, I was sentenced to a no-nonsense drug rehabilitation program. The program used urinalysis to monitor me and ensure that I was staying away from drugs. I also went to group and individual counseling in the evenings and on the weekends.

After about six weeks in the program, one of the counselors called me into his office.

His name was Robert O.

We sat face-to-face and he said, "David, you profess to be a Christian, right?"

"Yes sir," I replied.

He then said, "Tell me about your Jesus. Tell me about your God."

I proceeded to tell him everything I knew about Jesus and God. This amounted to a two- or three-minute telling of what I had learned as a child growing up in church. After a few minutes of patient listening, Robert raised his hand to interrupt me. "Stop!" Then, looking me straight in the eye, he said, "David, I suggest you find a new Jesus and a new God."

I was confused and offended, so I asked him why he said such a thing to me.

Softly, but very much to the point, and once again looking me dead in the eye, Robert O. said, "Well, David, what you claim to know now hasn't done you much good, has it?"

I opened my mouth to respond but no words came out. I was speechless. I had no defense. Robert O.'s words made me feel like I was the hole in a donut, like my whole religious life had been swept off the table and had crashed to the floor, broken into pieces.

The truth Robert O. spoke was so true I couldn't attack it or even get mad at him for saying it. In an instant, my religious pride evaporated into the nothing it had always been. The cold, impersonal, rule-keeping religious training I had grown up with had been of little good to me.

That conversation with Robert O. forced me to face my false beliefs, and it opened my heart and mind to know the

Source of Power which had given me life — the Source of Power that had protected me as I squandered my life — the Source of Power that offers us all the possibility of a new life worth living.

Honestly knowing God begins when we admit how little we know about him.

As absurd as it may sound, today I believe that my addictions are the second-best thing that has ever happened to me. While suffering the misery of my addictions, a pliable humility took hold inside of me. I'd had enough. I was defeated. I became desperate enough to try something new. I was prepared to trust something, Someone, more powerful than me.

WHAT WORKS

In Step Two of the Twelve Steps, "came to believe" expresses open-mindedness and faith. It refers to a willingness to look in a new direction for the power that can make a needed difference in our lives. "Came to believe" also suggests that we bring ourselves, physically and emotionally, to be with others who live consistently in recovery. We literally replace old environments that have been part of our destructive, addicted way of life with new ones that will help build a healthy, recovering life.

In my case, I "came to" (woke up out of the coma of denial) and became aware — physically, intellectually, and emotionally — of my life's ugly reality. I "came to" realize that the only reasonable thing to do was to surrender the silly belief that I was always in control. I "came to believe" that I needed to look beyond myself to find what I needed to live my life well.

In Operation Integrity, we make it a habit to admit our struggles to one another. We admit when we feel mentally and emotionally disconnected. We admit how we must stay away from our addictions at all costs if we are to have long-lasting recovery. Remembering the suffering of our addictions, and that we are powerless over our addictions, keeps us moving in a better direction.

But getting free from our addictions did not guarantee that our lives would be perfect. An important part of recovery is learning to be at peace even when life is hard. There was one thing we knew for sure: to continue the way we had been going almost guaranteed our destruction. It was in a community of shared struggle and confession that we found the honest, authentic faith that could build real integrity inside of us.

Faith begins when we stop claiming confidence only in ourselves.

When we failed, we shared our failures honestly with one or more of our partners in recovery. This taught us that we could build some integrity by admitting our failures to someone who understood. This is what a recovering fellowship is about: *we are loved for who we are and who we are becoming, regardless of our setbacks along the way.*

> *It was so bad we didn't think we were going to make it. We felt like we'd been sent to death row, that it was all over for us. As it turned out, it was the best thing that could have happened.*
>
> *~ 2 Corinthians 1:9 MSG*

Moving from Hopelessness to Hopefulness

I found tremendous help from other recovering sex addicts. When I felt the dismay of failure, they helped me feel hopeful, and not the hellish hopelessness I had felt when I was alone in my addictions. They even told me that they felt strengthened as they helped me. They even thanked me for calling to ask for their help!

In a recovering fellowship, the weak get stronger by confessing their truth, and the strong get stronger by hearing and helping the weak.

In Operation Integrity, we call "faith" *a hope-filled belief that empowers us to take the right step forward.* As we understand faith this way, it becomes an internal beacon for our soul. It is an antidote for addictive obsession, and proves itself by the way our lives get better over time.

When I saw others change, I came to believe that I could change too. Like a gift, a simple hope for life — faith — birthed open-mindedness inside of me. Faith appeared quiet and close. It came from outside of me, but worked its miracle within.

RELATIONSHIP — NOT RELIGION

As you already know, whatever I thought I had believed, and professed to others regarding God and/or religion, didn't matter much, because it wasn't authentic or practical enough to work day-to-day. Countless others have had a similar realization about their religious beliefs and opinions. Those who claimed no God were in trouble, and those who professed faith in God were in trouble too. We all ended up in the same place — addicted. What we needed above all else was effective help. Once we opened our minds and our hearts to new possibilities, we were ready to receive that help.

The concept of faith may offend those who consider themselves too smart to believe in God's existence. The mere idea of "faith" can threaten self-indulgent egos and self-mastered lives.

Some who came to Operation Integrity had once believed God was nothing more than a power-grabbing, hocus-pocus, religious magic show thought up by weak-willed people who were searching for power through religious distraction and human effort.

We might agree with them in one respect.

Any "god" created within the mind of man is not God.

Any "god" defined solely by human terms and descriptions serves only the dictates of someone's predetermined thinking, which is, to some degree, always flawed, shortsighted, and ignorant. If a religious belief originates in the mind of man, it is not from God.

It should also be said that indifference, complacency, self-sufficiency, and even religious defiance are understandable for those of us raised in religious environments that lacked nurturing love, were abusive, or didn't affirm the dignity God created within all people.

This is where we must be honest with ourselves. We all suffer from our own pride and prejudices which block us from discovering God in a way that makes a good difference in our lives. This is why we must seek God on his terms, not our own. We must ask God to tell us who he is, not who we expect him to be.

When we ask God honest questions, we find out who we really are.

REAL FAITH

Real faith is willing to accept any answer that helps us recover. It will not debate or try to win unnecessary arguments. Real faith understands that our need to live well is much greater than our need to be "right." Faith like this is authentic, and heals our wounded heart. It molds the humiliation of sexual addiction into an openness that maximizes our recovery, and builds a life worthy of appreciation and respect. Authentic faith transforms us from victims to survivors. It is the inner catalyst of spiritual revolution for every woman or man, be they religious-minded or not.

Faith like this is more common than you might realize.

When you turn the key to your car, what do you expect?

Power to start the engine.

When you flip a light switch, what are you looking for?

Power to light the room.

What do you want when you reach for your phone?

To make a connection.

We've learned to have faith in modern technology through personal experience, and we learn to have faith in God in much the same way.

This is how I discovered faith that empowers me to recover from my addictions. In varying ways, and with varying degrees of progress, I learned that I could trust in others — "higher powers," if you will — and in *the* Higher Power, God.

Let's pause for a moment to ponder.

If the thought of trusting God is troubling you, don't worry about it right now. There are lots of "higher powers" who can help if you let them. Relax! Let God help you learn to trust him. After all, if you think about it, isn't simply trusting in the process the first step of faith?

There are many in Operation Integrity who rejected God initially but they kept an open mind. They used other "higher powers," which helped them move into recovery. This, however, worked only as they remained honest with themselves and open-minded about God.

The true "Higher Power" will reveal himself to anyone who wants to know him.

Faith grows from a desperate, action-oriented hope. It flourishes with humility and openness. It is all about possibilities: the possibility that we can be free from sexual addiction, the possibility that our personality will be restored to sanity, and the possibility that God will be known in a deep, personal way. When you call for God, you don't need to know who to call for. He knows you are calling for him. There is no one else.

> *But there is One who has all power – that One is God. May you find Him now. Half measures availed us nothing. We stood at the turning point. We asked His protection and care with complete abandon.*
>
> *~ Alcoholics Anonymous, The Big Book, pg. 59*

As was said before, some in our fellowship were quite religious when they began their recovery work. They asserted that their way of life was "the way," the "right way," or the "only way." Yet no matter their religious claims, they became sexual addicts just like the rest of us. Their religious professions propped them up like religious scarecrows in a religiously popular bean field: faded, worn and lifeless, and unable to live beyond their spiritual needs and shortcomings.

It is spiritually dangerous to hide yourself in religion.

The truth of the matter is this: while *religious* addicts maintain well-intended commitments, and often speak eloquently about theology and God, their heartfelt religious experience is limited. Their so-called "faith" never grows beyond the boundaries of their own personal thinking and will never be sufficient for true spiritual living, as proven by their addictions.

Sex addicts are sex addicts, whatever their religion.

Lifeless, cold, rule-keeping religion often becomes an addiction to itself.

Religion is personally real only when it is a relational revolution that transforms a person's thoughts, feelings, actions, and their beliefs. Anything less is not true faith or true religion. But, having said this, we don't encourage anyone to leave their church or denomination. Where we failed to find authentic personal faith and live it out in an honest, sincere religious experience, many others from various churches have succeeded.

> *Instead of trusting in our own strength or wits to get out of it, we were forced to trust God totally — not a bad idea since he's the God who raises the dead!*
>
> ~ *2 CORINTHIANS 1:9 MSG*

Here are helpful questions to ponder:

Are your personal religious convictions successfully guiding you through life?

Are you free from the internal conflicts that result in addictions?

Has your "religion" been working for you?

If you answered yes to any of these, why are you reading this book?

Addictions of any kind prove that we need to become *spiritually simple* where we have been religiously pious, humble where we have been self-confident, honest where we have been self-deceived, and open-minded where we have been stubbornly convinced.

Before God will be anything to any of us, he will be the Savior of our needy soul.

When God touched me in his own time, I experienced a power that is deeply personal, beyond my comprehension, and impossible to explain. New ground was broken inside of me, and I hope the same for you.

> *When I was driven to my knees by alcohol, I was ready to ask for the gift of faith. And all was changed. Never again, my pains and problems notwithstanding, would I experience my former desolation. I saw the universe to be lighted by God's love; I was alone no more.*
>
> ~ *Bill Wilson*, The Grapevine, *January 1962*

> *In my own case, the foundation of freedom from fear is that of faith: a faith that despite all worldly appearances to the contrary, causes me to believe that I live in a universe that makes sense. To me, this means a belief in a Creator who is all power, justice and love; a God who intends for me a purpose, a meaning and a destiny to grow, however haltingly, toward his own likeness and image. Before the coming of faith I had lived as an alien in a cosmos that too often seemed both hostile and cruel. In it there could be no inner security for me.*
>
> ~ *Bill Wilson*, As Bill Sees It

Necessary Next Steps

As we said before, in Operation Integrity we believe that God and other "higher powers" can guide us to healthier living. Employers, parents, family, doctors, governments, and even law enforcement have some ability to help us if we let them. They can externally influence our behaviors in positive ways.

Here are some of the external resources we found helpful.

TWELVE STEP PROGRAMS AND SUPPORT GROUPS

We participated in Twelve Step support groups for sexual addiction. Sometimes we had other addictions, so we attended the appropriate fellowship for those areas of struggle: Alcoholics Anonymous for problems with alcohol, Narcotics Anonymous for drug abuse and drug addiction, Gamblers Anonymous for troubles with gambling, Overeaters Anonymous for compulsive and addictive eating, Workaholics Anonymous for workaholism, and so on.

We followed the suggestion of ninety meetings in ninety days, and avoided our addictions between meetings. We read and absorbed the literature, and sought time with other recovering men and women who inspired us to do the work of recovery just as they had. We have never stopped our Twelve Step meeting attendance, though the frequency of our attendance adjusted as our addictions healed.

SPONSORS AND MENTORS

We sought out a personal one-on-one relationship with a recovering sex addict whose life exemplified spiritual renewal — someone willing to guide us at a deep, personal level. We spoke to this person every day, maintaining our commitment to be honest with them. We followed their suggestions the best we could, realizing that their success could become our success only if we were willing to follow their guidance. When given assignments by our sponsor, we did the work the best we knew how. With our sponsor's help, we became proactive, which helped us avoid our addictions and begin building long-term recovery and healing.

PROFESSIONAL CARE

Some of us were in need of rehabilitation or treatment programs. Professional care is profoundly helpful when it's possible. We also told our personal physician if we ever abused medication or alcohol to ensure they gave us the best care. We also sought professional care through counseling, psychiatrists, and psychotherapists. These compassionate professionals offered indispensable expertise by helping us see further into ourselves and get to the honest core of our heart and mind.

HIGHER POWER — GOD AS WE UNDERSTOOD HIM

We humbly asked God to give us guidance and protection. We admitted how we often felt distant from him, and that we suffered because of how we misunderstood him. We admitted our doubts and concerns, and did our best to believe that God would meet us wherever we were. In time, we began to realize God was gently showing his loving nature to us.

Because we had come to understand that our addictions come from deep places inside of us, we asked God to meet us at the innermost place of our heart and mind. We discovered that God would do for us internally what others could only help us do externally. Yes, we saw paradox in the recovery process.

Healthy changes made to our outside, physical life help to heal us on the inside.

The healing of our inner life positively influences how we live our outer, physical lives.

Some of us felt that we had good reason to question God about the inequities and unfairness of life, and so we did. *Asking God honest questions and seeking honest answers is wonderfully normal.* God happily embraces us as we ask honest, tough questions.

I have learned over time that God is always ready to give me real answers and real solutions when I am ready to listen to and accept answers that I may not like.

Your faith doesn't need to be perfect or without a doubt to work. Be honest with God. Admit the doubt you feel. Ask him for his help. He will hear you, and he will help you.

> *Jesus said to him, "If you can believe, all things are possible to him who believes." Immediately the father of the child cried out and said with tears, "Lord, I believe; help my unbelief!"*
>
> *~ MARK 9:23–24 NKJV*

Some medical professionals have referred to addiction as a learned and inherited disease because of how behavioral and genetic traits are passed down in families. I call addiction the family disease. I also believe that addiction is the most human of all diseases because it reaches across the entire spectrum of human experience. It destroys bodily health, soundness of mind, emotional well-being, and spiritual development. If a person develops a physical disease such as cancer, there are treatments that may cure the cancer. If someone has mental or emotional difficulties, there are effective treatments through medication, psychotherapy, and support groups. If you want to recover from sexual addiction, you will have to address *all* of these, with priority number one being an authentic spiritual faith.

Once we are willing to seek the gift of spiritual renewal, our physical, emotional, and mental problems begin to heal as well.

> *And it is impossible to please God without faith. Anyone who wants to come to him must believe that God exists and that he rewards those who sincerely seek him.*
>
> *~ Hebrews 11:6 NLT*

PERSONAL REFLECTIONS

PERSONAL REFLECTIONS

A CHANGE OF HEART

We made a decision to turn our will and our lives over to the care of God as we understood Him.

~ STEP THREE FROM THE TWELVE STEPS

Teach me to do your will, for you are my God; may your good Spirit lead me on level ground.

~ PSALM 143:10

Commit to the LORD whatever you do, and he will establish your plans.

~ PROVERBS 16:3

Listen for GOD's voice in everything you do, everywhere you go; He's the one who will keep you on track.

~ PROVERBS 3:6 MSG

I spent the first forty years of my life trying to overcome one difficult thing after another, and failing much of the time. I struggled to make good grades in school, to make good decisions in life, and to be successful in my work. When my efforts ended poorly, which they so often did, I felt terribly abnormal and out of place. Just being me was painful, and the pain I felt triggered strong desires to escape what I was feeling. My addictions promised euphoric deliverance, but each time they brought less and less relief, and then they brought more pain. Over time, they eroded the most significant of my God-given dignities: the ability to make clear and healthy choices for myself.

But not anymore; things have changed.

Every day I stand at a crossroads. In one direction are the addictions that I loved so much, with their obvious allure and hidden destruction. In the other lies gut-wrenching openness and rigorous honesty.

At some point, we will all find ourselves at a crossroad like this.

Only honesty will tell us the right way to go.

OUR MOST SIGNIFICANT DECISION

Our unhealed addictions erode our ability to make healthy, life-enriching decisions. Nevertheless, there is one decision that will always be ours. It is the most significant decision of life.

Who will you trust? Who will you follow?

Always — or at the very least, most of the time — my intentions were sincere, and I thought my goals were clear. I certainly never intended to make a disaster of my life, yet I did. My willpower and ambition not only abandoned me, but drove me to become a prisoner to the very things I once thought I was entitled to. My addictions cost me the mental clarity I needed to make certain specific choices, and through negative consequences of bad decisions and bad behavior, I lost the opportunity to make other choices.

Our decision to surrender ourselves to God's care is far more personal and practical than religious. We surrender our will and life to God and accept his care, or we continue in the direction we've been going, and suffer more addicted death along the way. In one way or another, usually without consciously thinking about it, we all decide whether we are willing to trust God. Personally, I know that failing to trust God leaves me spiritually unprotected against my addictions — a life-threatening mistake for just about anyone to make.

NO HAND-ME-DOWN FAITH

There is no such thing as "hand-me-down faith." Important people in our life may offer an example of faith that we look to for inspiration, but a personal faith is our individual responsibility. At some point in our life, each of us will stand before God with our future in our own hands. And facing God in this life will make us face ourselves. This plays out in the decisions we make. Our daily decisions are how we choose what kind of person we will be and what our life will stand for.

When some of the men in the original fellowship of Operation Integrity first decided to entrust themselves to God, they experienced immediate, profound gratitude which they expressed with dramatic emotional outbursts. Others felt only quiet relief that their lives would change for the better. However it was felt or expressed, it was really quite simple: we knew we couldn't trust ourselves entirely, or manage our lives alone.

> *Trust in the LORD with all your heart; do not depend on your own understanding. Seek his will in all you do, and he will show you which path to take.*
>
> *~ PROVERBS 3:5–6 NLT*

We are all influenced by our culture, our friends, our families, our employers, and our coworkers. We are often judged by our appearance, our profession, and our social status. It is easy to let these outside influences dominate our inner life, but our inner will is the true center point for every woman and man alive. Everything we say or do is connected with our will. It is central to who we are and who we become. It is the doorway of decision through which we give or take in this world. Our will is the place inside of us where the never-ending question is asked: Will you be self-directed, or will you be God-directed?

As I worked through my personal recovery process, I began to see how my addictions had blinded me, and how I had been a slave to a hidden and addicted agenda. Without intending it, my goal had become very simple — to get the comfort I subconsciously thought I needed. My decisions were determined by what made emotional sense to me at the time. My will was enslaved, and I never knew it. Unwittingly, I had become my own god.

So, to find a better way to live, I had to make a new decision. In making this new decision, I also had to make a new goal. My new goal was to ask — continually ask — God to manage and care for that part of me that is made in his image, the part of me that is personally unique: my will.

> We had to quit playing God. It didn't work. Next, we decided that hereafter, in this drama of life, God was going to be our Director. He is the Principal; we are His agents. He is the Father, we are His children. Most good ideas are simple, and this concept was the keystone of the new and triumphant arch through which we passed to freedom.
>
> ~ ALCOHOLICS ANONYMOUS, THE BIG BOOK, PG. 62

God, I offer myself to Thee – to build with me and to do with me as Thou wilt. Relieve me of the bondage of self, that I may better do Thy will. Take away my difficulties, that victory over them may bear witness to those I would help of Thy Power, Thy love, and Thy way of life. May I do Thy will always!

~ *ALCOHOLICS ANONYMOUS,* THE BIG BOOK, *PG. 63*

Don't copy the behavior and customs of this world, but let God transform you into a new person by changing the way you think.

~ *ROMANS 12:2 NLT*

Once I had made the decision to turn my will over to God's care, I quickly learned that it was impossible to carry out that decision without turning my life over to God's care as well. This is because *the truest indicator of our will is the way we live our life.* Until we are willing to give our life to God entirely, which includes our circumstances, we have not surrendered our will.

My problem was that I had thought of my wants as if they were my needs. Also, because of my childhood wounds of abandonment, it was difficult for me to trust that someone other than me was sincerely concerned with my well-being. This caused me to make demands in ways I was not aware of. I wanted (or thought I *needed*) things to go my way. I wanted (*needed*, once again) other people to agree, to cooperate, and to assist me in getting what I thought was important. When I failed to get what I wanted, I became angry and resentful, which proved just how selfish I was, regardless of how good I assumed my intentions were. Then, without realizing it, I would punish others in one way or another. In so doing, I became intolerable to many people, who then cut me out of their lives. My misery grew all the more, and my addictions seemed irresistible once again.

Have you behaved like this?

Are you disagreeable and at odds with people close to you?

We can be relational mercenaries. We fight tooth and nail to get what we think is important. If pushing and shoving don't work, we *kill 'em with kindness* to mask our selfish motives. Sometimes we claim victory. Other times we strategically admit defeat so we can regroup to try and win once again.

TRUE SURRENDER

In true surrender, we quit fighting anyone or anything because we understand that the primary battle worth fighting is within ourselves. Because we admit that we are powerless over people, places, and things, we keep one simple goal: a faith that trusts in God's care.

> *You know you're surrendered to God when you rely on God to work things out instead of trying to manipulate others, force your agenda, and control the situation. You let go and let God work. You don't have to always be "in charge." Instead of trying harder, you trust more.*
>
> ~ RICK WARREN, THE PURPOSE DRIVEN LIFE

Sexual addiction is like a train wreck. Just because we slam on the brakes doesn't mean we won't crash and have the pieces of our lives come apart. Consequences already set in motion by poor decisions will likely play out to their natural conclusions. True surrender means that we are willing to face and accept the consequences that result from our actions.

In recovery, we also learn to make peace with an unfair world. We see people getting away with things we no longer get away with but sometimes wish we still could. At the same time, we find ourselves asking — or perhaps it is God asking — how many times did someone look at us and wonder why we were getting away with wrongdoing?

Truth is, no one gets away with wrongdoing for long.

Regardless of the consequences, our important work is to follow what we know to be God's will and leave others to do what they will, right or wrong.

God gives everyone the right to make their choices.

IT IS A PROCESS

A trusting faith in God, no matter how we may struggle with it, empowers us to live a process way of life. My process is mine, not yours. Your process is yours, not mine. We have little control over anything except our own willingness, which is the key that unlocks life-changing recovery. This does not guarantee the public success that most of us crave. *We are not called to be publicly successful; we are called to be personally and privately faithful.* With this humble mindset, we will make powerful contributions to the world around us.

> *God, grant me the serenity to accept the things I cannot change, the courage to change the things I can, and the wisdom to know the difference.*
>
> ~ *SERENITY PRAYER*

This life therefore, is not righteousness, but growth in righteousness, not health but healing, not being but becoming, not rest but exercise. We are not yet what we shall be, but we are growing toward it: the process is not yet finished but it is going on. This is not the end but it is the road; all does not yet gleam in glory but all is being purified.

~*MARTIN LUTHER*

"For I know the plans I have for you," says the LORD. "They are plans for good and not for disaster, to give you a future and a hope. In those days when you pray, I will listen. If you look for me wholeheartedly, you will find me. I will be found by you," says the LORD. "I will end your captivity and restore your fortunes. I will gather you out of the nations where I sent you and will bring you home again to your own land."

~ *JEREMIAH 29:11–14 NLT*

THE LARGER REALITY OF GRACE

God loves everyone, including all of us who became sexually addicted. God not only loves you, but he also delights in you and desires connection with you no matter what you have done. I am convinced of this because I have discovered it for myself. He revealed himself through the door of my desperately honest, open, and willing surrender.

A life-changing relationship with God is not a matter of how smart we are, but how sincere we are with him. He takes care of the rest. It is simple, it is effective, it is called grace.

Grace is God's gift of new life, no matter who you are, or what you have done.

When you are ready to receive it, God's grace will meet you right where you are. He will make his home in your heart, and from there, he will move into every aspect of your life —expanding his loving presence throughout your life.

I belief that all of us — whether we know it or not — long for this kind of grace-filled spiritual connection. To spiritually connect with a God who knows just what we need and who is eternally committed to love and care for us.

This is where Jesus connects with us for our redemption.

Jesus is the one who has always known God as the perfect Father. He reveals who God the Father is and what he is like. God may not be exactly what we want him to be, but he will always be everything we need him to be.

There is only one whose life displayed the perfection of purpose, whose death exemplified the perfection of love, and who lived again after death to prove and proclaim the perfection of loving power that changed individual lives and altered the course of world history. In Jesus, we will find someone whose destiny offered him all privileges, but he gave them up by his own choice, preferring to love others in surrender to his eternal Father — God.

Jesus refused to retaliate against those who sought to harm him. He even forgave those who killed him because he understood that they didn't understand who he was or what he was about. After giving up his life, Jesus lived again and appeared to his followers, proclaiming once and for all that he was capable of giving life to dying men and women. He invited those who were sinfully and socially ravaged — like many of us — to be spiritually close to him and to his Father.

Thank God, Jesus loves sexually addicted people like you and me.

> *"This is how much God loved the world: He gave his Son, his one and only Son. And this is why: so that no one need be destroyed; by believing in him, anyone can have a whole and lasting life. God didn't go to all the trouble of sending his Son merely to point an accusing finger, telling the world how bad it was. He came to help, to put the world right again. Anyone who trusts in him is acquitted; anyone who refuses to trust him has long since been under the death sentence without knowing it. And why? Because of that person's failure to believe in the one-of-a-kind Son of God when introduced to him."*
>
> *~ JOHN 3:16–18 MSG*

The life of Jesus will never be fully realized through a history lesson or a theological discussion. The place for Jesus' Spirit to live is inside of people who have been broken and abandoned, like we have been. We will be strengthened with his power as we trust in his care, and live out the hope-filled faith that he gives to us.

Jesus' life is our life; our life is his. God does not exist for us; we exist for God.

As we learn to see through the lens of eternity, everything will begin to make sense.

I am increasingly aware of the joy God gives, his excellent plan for me, and the assurance that both my life and the world around me are loved by him completely. The love of Jesus is changing my heart, and as my heart changes, my mind is changing too. The recovery I am receiving is not about rule-keeping, religious moralizing, and self-imposed corrections. I have experienced a complete change of allegiance, preferring an intimate relationship with God above my sexual addiction, above my life, above everything.

Jesus lived courageously, died lovingly, and lived again eternally so we can know that God eternally forgives you and me.

Are you ready to pray this prayer?

Dear God, I pray that I will learn to desire obedience more than blessing or comfort and to know that the greatest blessing in life is to live obedient to Your will. May I learn to better give up my will and find my complete and total satisfaction in Your will. My self-centeredness destroys me but seeking You and doing Your will brings life to me. Realizing this, I have decided that my mind, my heart, and my will, will be directed to You. I will find my purpose and identity in knowing You more personally and living more powerfully according to Your Spirit. Amen.

~ THE OPERATION INTEGRITY PRAYER

PERSONAL REFLECTIONS

PERSONAL REFLECTIONS

SAY HELLO TO YOU

We made a searching and fearless moral inventory of ourselves.

~ STEP FOUR FROM THE TWELVE STEPS

Let us examine our ways and test them, and let us return to the LORD.

~ LAMENTATIONS 3:40

Complain if you must, but don't lash out. Keep your mouth shut, and let your heart do the talking.

~ PSALM 4:4 MSG

"Stay alert; be in prayer so you don't wander into temptation without even knowing you're in danger. There is a part of you that is eager, ready for anything in God. But there's another part that's as lazy as an old dog sleeping by the fire."

~ MATTHEW 26:41 MSG

Addiction is a disorder of mental obsession that leads to destructive behavior that impacts a broad range of human experience. It grows from subconscious, self-defeating strategies that people use escape their pain. In everyday language, *addiction is the misguided notion that we can use something from outside of us to fix something wounded inside of us.*

Our acting-out behaviors made it possible to temporarily avoid painful feelings like inadequacy, fear, hopelessness, loneliness, and the feeling of being unwanted or unloved. We likely grew up with these painful feelings from childhood and have had them for so long we're not generally aware of them. Early in life, we learned to avoid our feelings through various kinds of intoxicating experiences. Along the way, we created a mood-altered life of make-believe and got lost in an addictive fantasy.

Anyone who wants to recover from their addictions must leave their fantasies behind and accept the honest reality of their life. Making an inventory of our feelings, beliefs, attitudes, and actions is a straightforward pursuit of this reality.

HAVE YOU BEEN FOOLING YOURSELF?

To find hearty, long-lasting recovery, you need to have a reasonable understanding of who you are, why you think the way you do, and why you do the things you do. This might even mean admitting how hopeless you feel or how weak you feel your faith to be.

Do you want to know God in a way that brings healing to you?

The place to start is with the truth about yourself.

If we procrastinate our self-revealing work, we delay a proven process of growing in honest relationship with God. All you need to do is to be as honest as you can. Your addictions are obvious evidence that you have struggled to be honest in the past, and tomorrow is not guaranteed. Your opportunity for recovery is to face yourself — today.

Most everyone in Operation Integrity will be quick to admit how they felt fearful and reluctant about making their personal inventory. It can feel like an impossible thing to do and we all needed help to make it happen. But as we became open-minded, we became willing to ask for the help we needed, and we got it. We got help from our sponsors, our mentors, and our counselors.

> *The moral inventory is a cool examination of the damages that occurred to us during life and a sincere effort to look at them in true perspective. This has the effect of taking the ground glass out of us, the emotional substance that still cuts and inhibits.*
>
> ~ *BILL WILSON,* AS BILL SEES IT

> *You want me to be completely truthful, so teach me wisdom.*
>
> ~ *PSALM 51:6 NCV*

WILLINGNESS EXPRESSED THROUGH ACTION

Willingness — expressed in action — is essential for all our efforts. By honestly recognizing our need for help and open-mindedly accepting help, we show the humble courage that is needed to grow our recovery. *Courage is a willingness to move forward in spite of our fear — to move in the very direction in which we are afraid.* Your personal inventory is your *courageous response-ability.* No one can do this for you but you. As a comforting reminder, let's remain confident that as we do our work of courage, God will help our hearts trust and our minds think in still more courageous ways.

A small amount of courage lived faithfully over time builds a beautiful life.

For God is working in you, giving you the desire and the power to do what pleases him.

~ PHILIPPIANS 2:13 NLT

The first step toward fortitude is dissecting our fears to find out what it really is that we're afraid of, then asking ourselves, is this fear legitimate? When we take the time to look at our fears in this way, most often, we'll find that the fear overlooks God's active presence.

~ GARY L. THOMAS, THE GLORIOUS PURSUIT

It is not your diligence; it is not your examination of yourself that will enlighten you concerning sin. Instead, it is God who does all the revealing. If you try to be the one who does the examining, there is a very good chance that you will deceive yourself.

~ JEANNE GUYON

Sexual addiction is not the cause of our moral failings, nor is it necessarily a moral failing in and of itself. Sexual addiction is a behavioral result of spiritual and emotional malnourishment. When making our moral inventory, we sift through our past and present to identify misguided, inaccurate beliefs, selfish thinking, and the unhealthy ways we tried to manage our emotions, all of which led to our addictive behavior. Our hidden nature is revealed through our external actions. Our addicted struggles will continue if our hidden nature and our actions are not faced and dealt with honestly.

"For you are so careful to clean the outside of the cup and the dish, but inside you are filthy—full of greed and self-indulgence! You blind Pharisee! First wash the inside of the cup and the dish, and then the outside will become clean, too."

~ MATTHEW 23:25–26 NLT

As I worked on my personal inventory, I began to see things inside of me that promoted my addictive thinking. I saw how frustrated I was, how lonely I had been most of my life, and how sad and angry I had become as an adult. My personal inventory was a practical, measurable commitment to clear the ground in preparation for the construction of a new person made by the loving design of God. This work brought objectivity. It helped bring my heart and mind into agreement with one another, and with God. As a result, I began to sense that I was becoming one of the most blessed of all men.

If we are painstaking about this phase of our development, we will be amazed before we are halfway through. We are going to know a new freedom and a new happiness. We will not regret the past nor wish to shut the door on it. We will comprehend the word serenity, and we will know peace. No matter how far down the scale we have gone, we will see how our experience can benefit others. That feeling of uselessness and self-pity will disappear. We will lose interest in selfish things and gain interest in our fellows. Self-seeking will slip away. Our whole attitude and outlook upon life will change. Fear of people and of economic insecurity will leave us. We will intuitively know how to handle situations which used to baffle us. We will suddenly realize that God is doing for us what we could not do for ourselves.

~ *ALCOHOLICS ANONYMOUS,* THE BIG BOOK, PG. *83–84*

FOCUS ON YOUR INVENTORY

You might find yourself obsessed over past harm someone has done to you.

I fell into this trap more than once.

While others may have caused you profound harm, it is essential, at least for now, that you concentrate on your mistakes, and not the mistakes of others. Each of us is responsible for dealing with our resentment in a healthy way. Let others work out their problems with God just as we are doing with ours. Their problems are not our job, and currently none of our business. If we fall into resentment, it will only cause us more harm. This is why it is important that you write about your resentments in your inventory. You can discuss them with your sponsor or mentor when the time is right.

My recovery partners and I worked through our personal inventories in different ways, but there were common characteristics. We faced questions posed to us by our sponsors and other people who were helping us in our recovery. Then we wrote our thoughts in journals, being sure to bravely answer every question asked. We wrote about our family history and any family memories we thought might be important. We wrote about the people who had harmed us. We wrote about the people we had harmed. We wrote about our sexual experiences, why we did the things we did, how we felt while doing them, and how we felt afterward. We wrote about love, what we desired love to be like, and how we had been disappointed by those we loved. We wrote it all. We wrote everything. The more we wrote, the more the questions unlocked the answers our hearts needed to know.

Here are some of the questions that we bravely answered:

- What are you angry about and why?

- How have others hurt you?

- Who hurt you? Was it parents, family members, people from church or school, neighbor, enemy, friend?

- Who and what are you afraid of?

- What was your first sexual experience?

- How old were you when you began the behaviors that turned into your sexual addiction?

- How have you violated your own sexual ethics?

- When did you first think you might be addicted sexually?

- How have your sexually addictive behaviors increased over time?

- How have you violated or objectified others sexually, personally, and socially?

- How have your sexually addictive behaviors impacted your spouse, your children, your health, and your career?

- How have you violated or objectified yourself?

- How have you abused those weaker than you?

- How have you been greedy?

- How have you been selfish?

- How have you been a hypocrite religiously, sexually, and socially?

- How have you expressed unwarranted pride?

- When and why do you feel self-pity?

- How have you manipulated others and your own thinking through self-pity?

- Why are you willing to sacrifice long-term health and sanity for short-term gratification?

- How and why have you minimized your mistakes and addictions?

- How have you exaggerated your successes?

- Have you minimized your successes? Why?

- What do you like about yourself?

- How have you blamed others for your difficulties?

- What do you feel guilty about?

- Is there anything that you are intentionally avoiding? What is it?

- What are you procrastinating about regarding your inventory?

- What do you not like about yourself?

- What do others like about you?

- Why do you lie?

I spent about a week doing my personal inventory, setting aside a specific time each day to do my work. Each time, I prayed for God to help me move through the fear and trepidation I was feeling. It helped to start with recent events and what was most troublesome to me. The more I wrote, the more I remembered, and the more I found clarity.

After a few days, I actually began to enjoy the experience of making my inventory. I wouldn't say that it was fun, but the working commitment to my own recovery, coupled with a sense of courageous accomplishment, made me grateful for the good work I felt happening inside of me. I became more open to God, and I found more inner strength. God took my willingness and made it possible for me to begin resolving my wounds once and for all. I saw that my failures and shortcomings could be remade into good and valuable assets.

If you sense anger when writing, write about it. If you sense fear, write about it. If you feel resentment, write it down. Don't leave anything out. Write everything down so that your sponsor/ mentor and counselor can talk it over with you face-to-face.

We don't need to be perfect in our work, but we do need to do the best we can. Let us begin by releasing our resentments, knowing that with God's help it will be possible to forgive every person who ever has hurt us.

This starts with forgiving ourselves.

To forgive is to set a prisoner free, and to discover all along the prisoner was you.

~ *CORRIE TEN BOOM*

PERSONAL REFLECTIONS

PERSONAL REFLECTIONS

GETTING REAL WITH OTHERS

We admitted to God, to ourselves, and to another human being the exact nature of our wrongs.

~ STEP FIVE FROM THE TWELVE STEPS

Confess your sins to each other and pray for each other so that you may be healed.

~ JAMES 5:16 NLT

Whoever conceals their sins does not prosper, but the one who confesses and renounces them finds mercy. Blessed is the one who always trembles before God, but whoever hardens their heart falls into trouble.

~ PROVERBS 28:13–14

Since we've compiled this long and sorry record as sinners (both us and them) and proved that we are utterly incapable of living the glorious lives God wills for us, God did it for us.

~ ROMANS 3:23 MSG

For forty years, I lived in the heart-forsaken land of emotional isolation. Raised in a large metropolitan area, lost and seemingly invisible among millions of people, I learned to exist in the world alone. I grew up to prefer life that way because I had never known any other way. It was the way of my family.

The rule in my family was that weakness would be ridiculed and punished if it was ever exposed. I grew up to believe that my *weakness* — whatever I thought that might be — had to be kept hidden behind a protective veneer of politeness and "Christian" civility. By the time I was a teenager, I was a master of avoiding both my inner emotions *and* anyone who might sense the loneliness I felt inside. I had no confidence in my upbringing. I doubted my worth. I survived and existed. Life was a living hell.

I was forty-one years old when I got help and began stopping my addictions — a big step in the right direction. In addition to stopping my self-destructive way of life, I also needed to learn how to come out of the emotional isolation I had learned as a child. I needed to learn how to live close with healthy people and have honest relationships with them. I am not sure which was scarier: the initial pain of turning away from my addictions, or the challenge of getting honest about myself with someone else.

A New and Better World

The work of ongoing recovery requires that we develop open and honest connections with ourselves, with God, and with others. This was intimidating to me at first, but as I persevered in doing the work, I began to feel a new, deeper closeness with good friends and a greater respect for myself. By admitting my faults and vulnerabilities to someone who could empathize with my experience, I was able to rise above the sense of isolation and condemnation I had grown up with. This *getting honest with another person* work reshaped my self-loathing into positive self-regard. The understanding I received helped me forgive myself for the bad decisions I had made when I was mired in the dark, emotional muck of survival mode. The people who listened to me without criticism or judgment taught me a lifelong lesson: *The greatest gift we can give to anyone is our presence, and our attentive, listening ear.*

But there was also more to this experience.

I started to laugh on occasion because I saw there was a humorous side to the things that once threatened my health and my safety.

Not everything in our past is tragedy.

As we move into honest relationships with people who are healthy enough to understand and care for us, we will be able to see the delight of human silliness in us all, and enjoy a light-hearted laugh which helps to heal our wounded souls.

> *"You're blessed when you're content with just who you are—no more, no less. That's the moment you find your-selves proud owners of everything that can't be bought."*
>
> *~ MATTHEW 5:5 MSG*

SAYING GOODBYE TO SECRETS

As we move deeper into healthier relationships, new feelings will emerge from inside of us. Not the fleeting, intoxicating feelings that our addictions brought. But deep, slow-moving emotions of peace, serenity, and solidarity with God and the world he created. As we say goodbye to our secrets, we become honest and free men and women, able to live true to who we really are.

> *We hide what we know or feel ourselves to be (which we assume to be unacceptable and unlovable) behind some kind of appearance which we hope will be more pleas-ing. We hide behind pretty faces which we put on for the benefit of our public. And in time we may even come to*

forget that we are hiding, and think that our assumed pretty faces is what we really look like.

~ Simon Tugwell, The Beatitudes: Soundings in Christian Traditions

At the beginning of my recovery work, admitting my faults was a miserable and desperate cry for connection because I somehow knew that secret-keeping shame had been slowly suffocating me. For others in Operation Integrity, admitting their faults was a relaxed, natural step toward better emotional and spiritual health. In either case, *transparent confession to people who understood our struggle was the way that we escaped our isolation.*

Getting real with God and another person is our chance to get supernatural help and human assistance linked together. It is our way of exposing and then loving the self-destructive impostor that hides inside of us.

Aligned to Truth

Admitting our wrongs to God does nothing to enlighten him. He knows our story better than we do; even the most sordid and gory details will not make him turn away. By admitting the exact nature of our wrongs to God, we stop running away, we turn around, and we walk straight toward God and sit ourselves before him to embrace his loving acceptance. This is our right place before God, our right place in the universe.

Which will you choose — to protect your secrets and be humiliated when they are exposed, or reveal them and accept the love and freedom you were created to know?

"The time is coming when everything that is covered up will be revealed, and all that is secret will be made known to all. Whatever you have said in the dark will be heard in the light, and what you have whispered behind closed doors will be shouted from the housetops for all to hear!"

~ *LUKE 12:2–3 NLT*

My false and private self is the one who wants to exist outside the reach of God's will and God's love — outside of reality and outside of life. And such a self cannot help but be an illusion.

~ *THOMAS MERTON IN JAMES FINLEY'S* MERTON'S PALACE OF NOWHERE

We used myriad forms of self-deception in the past to manipulate our view of ourselves. Much like the way Adam and Eve used fig leaves to avoid exposure, we hid in our self-deception (more of good ol' denial) to avoid facing the truth. But in recovery, we step out of our hiding places and allow our embarrassing vulnerabilities to be seen. This is how we move toward God. We do it in response to his constant invitation to become fully alive in him. Our intended identity — people made in the image of God — is reborn anew as we move toward the spiritual sound of God's call, and are vulnerable with him and with others.

Only now, however, is the evangelical church beginning to realize that without spiritual direction, without one-on-one or small group conversations where our lives are laid open in the presence of a person gifted to discern

the workings of our inner life, the disease of deception will not be cured. Without spiritual direction, millions of Christians will continue to walk the "OLD WAY," thinking they're on the path to knowing God well.

~ *Larry Crabb,* The Pressure's Off, *pg. 42*

A New Sheriff in Town

As we admit the exact nature of our wrongs to ourselves, the hidden idolatry that has dominated us begins to fall away. A revolutionary change has begun deep inside of us.

I had to be very direct with myself in order to turn my heart's loyalty away from my addictions and toward a loving God. What I admitted to myself was both a personal surrender to God, and a move of defiance against the self-absorbed faker and poser that I had grown up to become.

I give each of you this warning: Don't think you are better than you really are. Be honest in your evaluation of yourselves, measuring yourselves by the faith God has given us.

~ *Romans 12:3 NLT*

If we claim that we're free of sin, we're only fooling ourselves. A claim like that is errant nonsense. On the other hand, if we admit our sins—simply come clean about them—he won't let us down; he'll be true to himself. He'll forgive our sins and purge us of all wrongdoing. If we claim that we've never sinned, we out-and-out con-

tradict God—make a liar out of him. A claim like that only shows off our ignorance of God.

~ 1 JOHN 1:8–9 MSG

We will never heal ourselves, or solve all of the problems that we face. Grace is a lifesaving necessity for each and every one of us. As we accept our need for grace, we surrender our illusions and our egos. We surrender wars that are greater than our best efforts can ever win. The wars are over; they have already been won by God's grace.

I quit focusing on the handicap and began appreciating the gift. It was a case of Christ's strength moving in on my weakness. Now I take limitations in stride, and with good cheer, these limitations that cut me down to size—abuse, accidents, opposition, bad breaks. I just let Christ take over! And so the weaker I get, the stronger I become.

~ 2 CORINTHIANS 12: 7–10 MSG

One of the greatest returns that our honesty will bring is when we hear someone in our fellowship say, "Me too."

A timely "Me too" reminds us of how others have suffered similar shortcomings and sins, just like we have. This identifying connection brings healing to our perspective. It further delivers us from the power of our secrets and changes the way we relate with others. When people give the power of love through an understanding ear, compassion soaks in deeply, washing away the poison of self-hatred and condemnation. To not risk honesty, to not trust, to not heal, to not become relationally and emotionally whole, leaves us alone and at the mercy of sexual addiction.

When we lose the foundation of trusted relationship, we have no one to trust but ourselves, and yet it is the self that feels most foolish and incapable of making safe and solid decisions. We are in a trap. We are cut off from others. We hate our desire. We want relief from our pain. We want someone to care and comfort us, but we also want justice, vengeance. The dark desire to make our betrayer pay places us in a strange position of being both a victim and an abuser.

~ Dan B. Allender, The Healing Path

What comes into our minds when we think about God is the most important thing about us.

~ A. W. Tozer

Next Steps

You might wonder, *Who am I going to tell my secrets to?*

Here are some suggestions that helped me.

Pick someone of the same gender, perhaps from your list of "higher powers." A clergyperson often works well, but not always. A counselor or medical professional can be helpful in matters related to addiction. Most of all, seek someone you believe is trustworthy — someone who will honor your confidentiality. Look for someone who believes in your ability to recover based on the strength of a loving God. Someone who has suffered their own addictions, and is in recovery, is usually a good choice. I was fortunate to find someone in long-term recovery for his own sexual addiction, and he also exemplified the love of Jesus. I hope you find someone like this because your listener will become your advocate in recovery, like Jesus is your advocate with God. Most of all, you'll want someone who won't ignore your self-deception or dishonesty, but who will also be understanding because they recognize the God-given goodness inside of you.

When you find the person, share with them what you need to do and why you feel they have something to offer you. Be straightforward and direct. It is important that you tell them you have become addicted sexually and that you need help from God and from others. Tell them of your desire to grow your faith, and of your need to have honest relationships with others.

Be respectful when asking for their time. Explain that it may take more than one appointment. Conversations like these cannot be rushed if they are to be effective. I also suggest that you tell them what you have thought about yourself, others, and God. Do your best to avoid discussing the faults of others. Stick to the facts about yourself. Don't minimize, and don't exaggerate.

Tell the truth. It will confound your enemies and astound your friends.

~ MARK TWAIN

Once I had spoken with someone else about my addictions and my life, I took time for personal reflection. I drove to a place of solitude and thanked God for the courage he had given me. I saw how God had been in the midst of the conversation I'd had with this other person. In the solitude, I realized I sense God's love most closely when I show up with the honest truth about myself. I enjoyed sitting quietly and peacefully, experiencing my body, my mind, and my heart at peace with one another. The angst-filled tightness in my chest that I had suffered since childhood was nearly all gone. In its place was a feeling that the world is good, and that I was a valuable part of it. I had been changed, and my experience of living with other people had been changed too.

Yet I also knew that my recovery journey was not finished, and that I was still capable of addictive self-destruction. I asked God to help me continue growing in honesty with him, myself, and with others. Most importantly, I knew that I didn't have to bear the burden of my faults and sins alone.

God is always working one loving step ahead of us.

PERSONAL REFLECTIONS

PERSONAL REFLECTIONS

DISCOVERING NEW DESIRE

We became entirely ready to have God remove all these defects of character.

~ STEP SIX FROM THE TWELVE STEPS

Humble yourselves before the Lord, and he will lift you up.

~ JAMES 4:10

I'll never forget the trouble, the utter lostness, the taste of ashes, the poison I've swallowed. I remember it all—oh, how well I remember—the feeling of hitting the bottom. But there's one other thing I remember, and remembering, I keep a grip on hope: GOD's loyal love couldn't have run out, his merciful love couldn't have dried up.

~ LAMENTATIONS 3:19–22 MSG

Just think how much more the blood of Christ will purify our consciences from sinful deeds so that we can worship the living God. For by the power of the eternal Spirit, Christ offered himself to God as a perfect sacrifice for our sins.

~ HEBREWS 9:14 NLT

The journey of recovery has given me a perspective from which I consider myself fortunate because I've had so many addictions. The suffering they caused taught me things many people will never understand. My drunkenness, drug use, and the pathetic, emotionally dependent way I survived my life showed me beyond doubt that I needed deep interpersonal healing, and that was I powerless to heal myself alone.

I also realized that the way my addictions to *things* changed over time proved that *things* were not my core problem. My problem was me! Namely, the way I thought about my life, God, and other people. As this came into focus, I realized that as far back as I could remember, I had been miserable and shamefully dissatisfied with who I was. My best intentions and my heartbreaking failures had fused together in a way that made me entirely ready to be remade into a fundamentally different kind of person.

DISSATISFACTION AND DESIRE ARE GIFTS FROM GOD

For someone struggling with addiction, dissatisfaction with the current condition of their life can be a gift because it can motivate them to change. Dissatisfaction pushes us beyond our complacency. If we pay attention to it, dissatisfaction will build desire within us — a desire that compels us to take action.

> *"Blessed are those who hunger and thirst for righteousness..."*
> ~ *MATTHEW 5:6*

Once I came to terms with it, the dissatisfaction I felt inside motivated me to do whatever I had to do to make things better. I was no longer willing to sit in the center of my problems, assuming things would change by themselves. I knew I had to change before my circumstances would change.

Until we become discontent with the rigors of trying to escape our powerlessness, we will live locked into the present status quo. If we are fully at home in our situation, then we will not ponder a better tomorrow. Discontent is the mother of invention. Discontent is holy when it compels us to dream of redemption.

~ Dan B. Allender, The Healing Path, pg. 84

Healthy desire grows from the untenable reality of our corrupted life when it is compared side by side with a better life. *The dissatisfaction you feel is authentic and good.*

As you honor it, it rewards you with a compelling desire for a better future — not only a future where you are recovering from sexual addiction, but one where you are free in every way.

We don't want to be healed from just our suffering; we want our entire character reworked by the perfect design of God.

No matter what we do or where we hide, we can't escape our essential design. We long to be free of shame's restraints, immersed in the passion of giving and receiving. We long to live a sacrificial life that matters today and tomorrow.

~ Dan B. Allender, The Healing Path,
pg. 107

BALANCE AND RESPONSIBILITY

One of the challenges in long-term recovery is how to have a healthy balance of our needs for love, personal security, and social inclusion. Trauma and addiction distort our understanding of these, so we often misunderstand their importance in our lives.

Perhaps we grew up believing that no one would care for us when we were in need, so to protect ourselves from more heartbreak, we didn't accurately communicate our needs to someone who could help. Or we expected others to magically meet our needs because we were too wounded to take healthy responsibility for them. Either way, we grew up denying our needs or obsessed with getting them satisfied any way possible.

Loneliness compounds itself when our personal needs are not met in healthy ways. As a result, we suffer the same self-obsession that fueled our addictions.

Persistent feelings of inferiority or superiority, grandiose, unrealistic expectations, selfish intentions, or secret motives are symptoms of an inner problem. If we think that our demands must be met, or that it is bad to feel pain or have difficulty, or that others must make us happy, the reality of this self-obsessed thinking shows that we remain the wounded center of our lives.

Self-centeredness is ground zero for character defects.

It is highly destructive, even when it is unintentional.

But this can change as we do our recovery work. Self-centeredness falls away as we face it and reach out to God and others in honest confession. As we do this, we'll learn not to make quick, knee-jerk assumptions about what is best for us. Impulsive thoughts and decisions get us into trouble almost all the time.

Just because our head sits on our shoulders does not mean it is always our friend.

It is ever important to pause, and pray, and to ask for guidance.

Since most of us are born with an abundance of natural desires, it isn't strange that we often let these far exceed their intended purpose. When they drive us blindly, or we willfully demand that they supply us with more satisfactions or pleasures that are possible or due us, that is the point at which we depart from the degree of perfection that God wishes for us here on earth. That is the measure of our character defects or, if you wish, of our sins.

~ *Alcoholics Anonymous, Twelve Steps and Twelve Traditions, pg. 65*

Recovery with Christ at the center brings ever-increasing opportunities to make good choices leading to abundant life. But! There is always one absolutely wrong choice! And that is to make yourself the center of your own world. Our character defects and our sins thrive when we try to play god. On the other hand, as we intentionally focus our minds and hearts on God, we naturally become more willing to let go of our character defects and the habitual sinfulness that has held us back. Trusting God in even the smallest of ways builds growth in willingness. Growth in willingness is growth in faith. God is pleased with willingness and faith; no matter how small it may be, he will grow it even more.

"Faith as small as a mustard seed."

~ *Matthew 17:20*

EMOTIONAL TRIGGERS

Hidden, painful emotions were the unseen reasons that we longed to escape the pain of our inner reality. The behaviors of our addictions were the ways we avoided our inner reality, but they became our prison. Our character defects are the building blocks of our prison walls, and our self-centeredness is the cement that holds our prison walls together.

Today, I have a better understanding of how my character defects began innocently when I was a child. They were my means of survival. I lied to protect myself. I manipulated to get my needs met. I hid my painful feelings to avoid embarrassment and shame. I rationalized my questionable behavior to escape a reality that was more than I could handle. My character flaws developed as broken, ineffective tools used to minimize pain. They were the secret, hidden strategy — secret and hidden even to myself — that I used to take care of myself because I thought no one else would.

Early in recovery, I sometimes felt afraid of what life would be like without my character defects. When I felt that something — like my binge overeating — would make me feel better, I mourned the thought of not indulging when I felt the urge. Fortunately, my sponsor and recovery partners helped me understand that though fearing the loss of coping mechanisms and bad habits was understandable, it was necessary that I let them go so I could move on down the path of recovery.

As we make the daily decision to turn our will and our life over to the care of God, the self-centered cement that holds our addictions together begins to lose its strength. But this doesn't mean that we'll be immune to internal conflict.

We can't avoid difficult emotions; they will come and go like the wind.

The best thing is to face the reality of our difficult emotions, and speak honestly to our sponsor or a trusted recovery partner about them. Healthy relational interaction helps release the pain of difficult emotions, so that our painful emotions are less likely to trigger destructive behaviors once again.

THE GIFT OF GRATITUDE

In my early recovery, I began to feel a deep release of the pressure and stress that I'd had inside of me. I learned healthier ways to cope, without taking drugs, drinking alcohol, or being sexual in ways that made me feel bad about myself. The process taught me to trade in my troubling, self-destructive thoughts and emotions for the humble gift of gratitude.

Gratitude posts a strong, loving guard at the door of our hearts. Gratitude helps us be thankful for life as it is, and not mourn for how we wish it to be.

> *O Israel, if you will truly return to me and absolutely discard your idols, and if you will swear by me alone, the living God, and begin to live good, honest, clean lives, then you will be a testimony to the nations of the world, and they will come to me and glorify my name.*
>
> ~ *JEREMIAH 4:1–2 TLB*

I also noticed this shift toward gratitude in others. Gratitude was evidence that we had taken healthy steps forward. Gratitude also connected us even more closely with other recovering people. Strengthened by gratitude, we again looked to our sponsors, our mentors, and our counselors for more guidance. They helped us keep moving away from our addictions and avoid new addictions along the way.

The dual diagnosis of addiction is becoming more common in rehab centers and some Twelve Step fellowships. Common co-addictions can be abuse of food and destructive eating or un-healthy food restriction, compulsive spending, gambling, work-ing too much, alcohol and other drug addictions, and even the misuse of prescription medications. *Religion can become an ad-diction as well.* We may also become obsessed with certain people and specific outcomes we think are necessary in a relationship. This may reflect how we are addicted to controlling the lives of others.

Something to remember: failure to recognize a destructive behavior (denial, once again) can potentially trigger relapse into sexual addiction. *This is because all addictions at their core are a destructive relationship with a mind- or mood-altering substance or experience that expresses itself in destructive behavior.*

If you think you have a problem with a substance, it's es-sential that you get help. This is true even if it's a drug your doctor has prescribed. If that's the case, your doctor is the first person you should ask for help. If you are drinking destructively, seek professional help and call Alcoholics Anonymous. Similar guid-ance holds true for any addictive behavior. The longer you wait to get help, the more you will suffer.

> "*Your GOD is present among you, a strong Warrior there to save you. Happy to have you back, he'll calm you with his love and delight you with his songs. The accumulated sorrows of your exile will dissipate. I, your*

God, will get rid of them for you. You've carried those burdens long enough."

~ *ZEPHANIAH 3:17–18 MSG*

BECOMING AWARE

A suggestion that helped me was to review the journal notes I had made after I admitted the exact nature of my wrongs to someone else. My journal notes revealed how my hidden beliefs had been inconsistent with my obvious, conscious beliefs. This created conflict in the way I lived. The more I recognized the conflicts in my life, the more my character defects appeared in bold print.

These questions (and their answers) helped me:

- Have I had difficulty admitting my need for help? *Pride.*

- Have I been in debt or preferred my desires over someone else's needs? *Greed.*

- Have I gotten mad because someone else was more privileged than me? *Envy.*

- Have I lived my life in a fearful way? *Trusting myself more than God.*

- Have I compared my insides with the outward appearance of others? *Self-objectification.*

- Have I enjoyed the attractive appearance of another while ignoring their feelings? *Lust and objectification.*

- Have I wanted to please others more than God? *Approval seeking.*

- Have I been frustrated when others didn't live the way I wanted them to? *Controlling.*

- Have I feared being alone? *Emotional dependence on others.*

- Have my family or I suffered from my long work schedule? *Being a workaholic.*

- Have I felt the need to keep certain facts about myself a total secret? *Dishonesty.*

- Have I had habits of unhealthy eating? *Nutritional self-abuse.*

- Have I procrastinated doing things that should be done? *Laziness.*

- Have I believed my life would change without me changing? *Fantasy thinking.*

Never Forgetting

As we make our progress in recovery, it's easy to think that we are "recovered." This may lead to complacency and blind us to the insidious nature of sexual addiction.

Perhaps your spouse has come back, your boss is happy with your work, and you're paying your bills on time. These are important, of course, but to keep recovering from our addictions, we must not ignore work that still needs to be done.

Honest questions guide us to honest answers.

- Have your selfish actions *ever* turned out well for you in the long run?

- How have your character defects impacted the lives of others?

- Are you *sincerely* kind to others, or is your kindness a way to hide your selfish motives?

- Do you think about how God is working in your life?

- Do you ponder the progress you're making, the fellowship you have discovered, and the better life you have today?

Questions like these are gifts from your loving God.

He has been working to help you even before you recognized your need.

Good friend, don't forget all I've taught you; take to heart my commands. They'll help you live a long, long time, a long life lived full and well.

~ PROVERBS 3:1–2 MSG

To admit discontent and hunger for redemption requires that we face our part in the problem and compels us to yearn and dream of more.

~ DAN B. ALLENDER, THE HEALING PATH, PG. 85

We suggest that you keep a journal, or carry a small notebook with you throughout the day. Your journal entries will help you see how God is doing miraculously more than you could have done on your own.

I am filled with awe by your amazing works. In this time of our deep need, help us again as you did in years gone by. And in your anger, remember your mercy.

~ *Habakkuk 3:2 NLT*

Reversing the Past

It is a vitally good and wonderful thing to accept the humbling fact that we cannot fix our shortcomings on our own. But we can change the behaviors that reinforce them. Letting go of the shortcomings and flaws in our character is never passive. Change inside of us is a divine interaction between God's grace and our choices and actions. The healthy changes we make build healthier thinking and emotional responses.

Motion changes emotion!

If our old way of thinking and acting didn't work well in the past, our experience shows that it won't work now. It's time we try something different. When we realize we are reacting with a character defect, or suffering an addicted thought or impulse, we have the opportunity to do something other than what our addicted instincts urge us to do.

It will take practice, but with reasonable effort and commitment, and perhaps a few failures along the way — which we'll share with someone in our recovery fellowship — the changes to our thinking, feeling, and living will happen quite quickly. Those who have come from religious backgrounds often call this repentance, and that is what it is. Grassroots, down-and-dirty, rubber-meets-the-road repentance. It's an about-face. It's turning and going the other way.

A simple definition of repentance is to change one's mind.

And so I insist—and God backs me up on this—that there be no going along with the crowd, the empty-headed, mindless crowd. They've refused for so long to deal with God that they've lost touch not only with God but with reality itself. They can't think straight anymore. Feeling no pain, they let themselves go in sexual obsession, addicted to every sort of perversion. But that's no life for you. You learned Christ! My assumption is that you have paid careful attention to him, been well instructed in the truth precisely as we have it in Jesus. Since, then, we do not have the excuse of ignorance, everything—and I do mean everything—connected with that old way of life has to go. It's rotten through and through. Get rid of it! And then take on an entirely new way of life—a God-fashioned life, a life renewed from the inside and working itself into your conduct as God accurately reproduces his character in you.

~ EPHESIANS 4:19–24 MSG

PERSONAL REFLECTIONS

PERSONAL REFLECTIONS

A NEWER YOU

We humbly asked Him to remove our shortcomings.

~ STEP SEVEN FROM THE TWELVE STEPS

Don't copy the behavior and customs of this world, but let God transform you into a new person by changing the way you think. Then you will learn to know God's will for you, which is good and pleasing and perfect.

~ ROMANS 12:2 NLT

And we are confident that he hears us whenever we ask him for anything that pleases him. And since we know he hears us when we make our requests, we also know that he will give us what we ask for.

~ 1 JOHN 5:14–15 NLT

You can be sure that God will take care of everything you need, his generosity exceeding even yours in the glory that pours from Jesus.

~ PHILIPPIANS 4:19 MSG

Early on I realized there would always be more to learn if I was going to keep moving away from my addictions. Fortunately, I had met other people who were consistently working the addiction recovery process. One of the helpful things they shared was to think of *humility,* or the word *humbly,* as an attitude that follows God's will over our own. This sounds simple, but I have not always done it well. Nevertheless, adopting this simple attitude for myself marked a deep shift in my soul.

A healthy understanding of humility was new to me. As a child, I had learned a distorted meaning of the word. From my parents' example, I grew up confusing humility with self-loathing and self-hatred. Subconsciously I believed it was *humble* not to like myself. By grade school, I believed my feelings of self-pity and defeatism were evidence of humility. This wasn't my parents' intention, of course, but their confusion confused me.

Today, when I'm thinking *humbly,* I'm thinking about how amazing, good things happen to unamazing people like me. Humility helps me know that life's difficulties will eventually make sense, so I can be at peace even when my world is turning upside down. On the other hand, when I choose to go my own way, which I sometimes do without even realizing it, my self-abusive thoughts return. I struggle with the silly notion that life revolves around me. Then, the old feelings of fear and angst return.

Low self-esteem or a negative self-image is never humility.

Low self-esteem hits us hardest when we forget the love God expresses for us in Scripture.

Misconceptions of God cause spiritual and emotional blindness, and this can cause us to betray ourselves without knowing it. Self-betraying thinking brings self-destructive behavior, which works hand in glove with our addictions. And because denial is the core stronghold of addiction, we are often blind to it. We return to rationalizing our destructive behavior, minimizing the damage our behaviors caused, and making excuses for why we did wrong.

Recovery is not possible when we make excuses not to change. Even when our excuses are rooted in the way we were raised. We are the only ones who can take real responsibility for our lives. Yes, this requires humility.

> *For just so long as we were convinced that we could live exclusively by our own individual strength and intelligence, for just that long was a working faith in a Higher Power impossible. This was true even when we believed God existed. We could actually have earnest religious beliefs which remained barren because we were still trying to play God ourselves. As long as we placed self-reliance first, a genuine reliance upon a Higher Power was out of the question. That basic ingredient of all humility, a desire to seek and do God's will, was missing.*
>
> ~ ALCOHOLICS ANONYMOUS, TWELVE STEPS AND TWELVE TRADITIONS, *PG. 72*

FACING THE FACTS

My experience with healthy humility began when I first admitted the reality of my addictions. I grew in humility as I worked through my personal inventory and began to view myself more honestly. The work of doing a personal inventory makes it possible for us to humbly "own" the facts about ourselves. As we honestly own the facts about our choices and lives, we'll be less inclined to minimize our struggles, rationalize our destructive actions, or ignore the pain others have suffered because of our poor choices.

We are not all-powerful. We do not control ourselves all of the time, nor do we control other people any of the time. Humility understands this. Humility gives us the eyes to see how God will change who we are, the way we think, the way we experience and embrace our emotions, and the way we live. As we are changed on the inside, our lives change on the outside.

I have learned to think of healthy character development as a personal responsibility *and* a gift at the same time. It is my responsibility to admit my character defects in the most honest way I know how. Growth is a gift that God gives as we do this humble work. When I notice my character defects in my thoughts and actions, I choose to change my thinking and my actions to receive more of the gift of growth. Each time I do this, the shortcomings in my character wither and are replaced with healthy growth.

Our character defects heal most effectively when we change the way we live.

Our priorities will change in the process. We will develop a humility that desires obedience more than blessing and character growth more than comfort — all so that we may help and not hinder the loving work of God.

The greatest blessing for any sex addict is to live free from addiction, fully aligned with the will of a loving God.

> *So humble yourselves under the mighty power of God, and at the right time he will lift you up in honor. Give all your worries and cares to God, for he cares about you.*
>
> *~ 1 Peter 5:6–7 NLT*

> *A great turning point in our lives came when we sought for humility as something we really wanted, rather than as something we must have. It marked the time when we could commence to see the full implication of Step Seven.*
>
> *~ Alcoholics Anonymous, Twelve Steps and Twelve Traditions, pg. 75*

I cannot count how many times — usually motivated by guilt and religiosity — I asked God for patience, only to get angry when patience didn't show up when I wanted it to. Obviously this proved I wasn't really interested in being more patient. What I really wanted was to feel relief from the tension I felt at the time. With what I know now, it is more helpful to admit to God, and to someone else, that I am often an impatient person. I confess that I sincerely want to live in a more patient way.

Saying, "Dear God, please make me more patient," sounds good, but we might miss the subtle implication that we are holding God responsible for our impatience. But when we say, "Dear God, I am an impatient person, and I need your help to change," we offer the truth about ourselves, and we accept responsibility for our impatience. *Changes in our circumstances are optional; changes in our character are necessary.* We let go of our pride to do this, inviting God to act according to his purpose in our lives.

> *My Creator, I am now willing that you should have all of me, good and bad. I pray that you now remove from me every single defect of character which stands in the way of my usefulness to you and my fellows. Grant me strength, as I go out from here, to do your bidding. Amen*
>
> *~Seventh Step Prayer, Alcoholics Anonymous,* The Big Book

As we admit the failures we most want to hide, we will see how God has been patiently waiting to make a deeper, life-transforming connection with us. Though we have been previously ruled by lusts, addictions, and other people, we are becoming the kind of men and women who admit our shortcomings, and, in doing so, we become even more filled with the transforming spirit of Christ.

> *"God's kingdom is like a treasure hidden in a field for years and then accidentally found by a trespasser. The finder is ecstatic—what a find!—and proceeds to sell everything he owns to raise money and buy that field."*
>
> ~ Matthew 13:44 MSG

> *So in terms of what every man needs most crucially, all man's power is powerless because at its roots, of course, the deepest longing of the human soul is the longing for God, and this no man has the power to satisfy.*
>
> ~ Frederick Buechner, The Magnificent Defeat, pg. 33

The Source of Our Strength

God did not create the problems in our character, but now, audacious as it is, we are asking him to heal them. That God is delightfully willing to do it is the humble glory we discover. As we surrender our lives, and humbly ask God to remove our shortcomings, we connect with his strength in a way unlike we've ever known before. With God's help, and the help of others, we will receive the endurance, the stamina, and the strength to continue to let go of our addictions, and our character defects. Just like everything else in our lives, we entrust our character to God. The timing God chooses in removing our shortcomings serves his purposes. The best thing we can do is accept the pain and consequences we have caused as learning opportunities, so that we can learn and benefit from our experiences once and for all.

Sometimes we won't do as well as we hope. We will face situations where we must apply our best efforts while trusting God, even though our best efforts failed before. Failure with honest effort produces sorrow and the discouraging feeling that we may never overcome our lusts. So let's make peace with the reality of setbacks and the possibility of failure. Setbacks and failure are an opportunity to turn to God once again as the loving source of our strength.

> *For the kind of sorrow God wants us to experience leads us away from sin and results in salvation. There's no regret for that kind of sorrow.*
>
> ~ *2 CORINTHIANS 7:10 NLT*

> *We can accept God's good gifts too easily. Grace can be accepted only when we face our own inabilities. Forgiveness can be embraced only when we lay bare our wrongdoing, and hope can be imparted only when we face the reality of our own despair.*
>
> ~ *CHARLES RINGMA*

ARE YOU WILLING?

When I realized that I was holding on to a character defect, I admitted the fear that I felt in letting it go, as well admitted the stubborn doubts that were rampant in my addiction-warped point of view. I admitted these things to myself, to God, and to another person. Without religious bravado, or proclaiming personal confidence, I simply asked God to help me let go of everything that stood between me and a closer relationship with him.

The moment we say, "No, never!" our minds close against the grace of God. Delay is dangerous, and rebellion may be fatal. This is the exact point at which we abandon limited objectives, and move toward God's will for us.

ALCOHOLICS ANONYMOUS, TWELVE STEPS AND TWELVE TRADITIONS, PG. 69

The release of our character defects starts with acting as if God has already equipped us to live beautifully without them. This means we take the opposite action we would have taken if we were acting *with* our character defect. We reverse course, *acting as if* God has given us everything we need. If we want to be like Jesus, a good place to start is admitting our struggle and failure, and living in faith as if we *are* becoming like Jesus.

It is obvious what kind of life develops out of trying to get your own way all the time: repetitive, loveless, cheap sex; a stinking accumulation of mental and emotional garbage; frenzied and joyless grabs for happiness; trinket gods; magic-show religion; paranoid loneliness; cutthroat competition; all-consuming-yet-never-satisfied wants; a brutal temper; an impotence to love or be loved; divided homes and divided lives; small-minded and lopsided pursuits; the vicious habit of depersonalizing everyone into a rival; uncontrolled and uncontrollable addictions; ugly parodies of community. I could go on. This isn't the first time I have warned you, you know. If you use your freedom this way, you will not inherit God's kingdom. But what happens when we live God's way? He brings gifts into our lives, much the same way that fruit appears in an orchard—things like affection for others, exuberance about life, serenity. We develop a willingness to stick with things, a sense of compassion in the heart, and a conviction that a basic holiness permeates things and people. We find ourselves involved in loyal commitments, not needing to force our way in life, able to marshal and direct our energies wisely.

~ *GALATIANS 5:19–23 MSG*

Personal Reflections

PERSONAL REFLECTIONS

SEEING THE WORLD AROUND US

We made a list of all persons we had harmed, and became willing to make amends to them all.

~ STEP EIGHT FROM THE TWELVE STEPS

"Do to others as you would like them to do to you."

~ LUKE 6:31 NLT

"And why worry about a speck in your friend's eye when you have a log in your own? How can you think of saying to your friend, 'Let me help you get rid of that speck in your eye,' when you can't see past the log in your own eye? Hypocrite! First get rid of the log in your own eye; then you will see well enough to deal with the speck in your friend's eye."

~ MATTHEW 7:3–5 NLT

"For if you forgive other people when they sin against you, your heavenly Father will also forgive you. But if you do not forgive others their sins, your Father will not forgive your sins."

~ MATTHEW 6:14–15

Almost everything that we say and do in life affects those around us. It might be big or small, and may not be realized in the moment, but our attitudes and our actions solicit response, reaction, and consequence. My sponsor drove this point home to me — the reality of my social responsibilities. With his gentle but firm help, I came face-to-face with my shortcomings and did my best not to look away. I realized how I had lived primarily for myself, and other people had suffered because of it. Today, I do my best to be more aware of my shortcomings, especially how they affect others.

My shortcomings illuminate my need for God; they point to my need for his grace and strength.

Life in recovery is the best life I have ever known. But nevertheless, as good as I feel, there remains a deep, nagging sense that I have unfinished business with others. Also, my sponsor and mentors urge me to be cautious and circumspect. They remind me that the practical everyday reality of my *new life in Christ* will be short-lived if I forget how I have negatively impacted the lives of others.

Don't Waste Your Recovery

When we forget our failures, when we compare our virtues favorably with the faults of others, when we try to claim imaginary, nonexistent success, or when we trade an honest spiritual relationship with God for orchestrated religious pretending, the most insidious kind of self-centeredness develops: self-righteousness. When we forget how we have hurt others, we become piously religious, self-absorbed, and self-satisfied. When we forget our failures, we become the hypocritical *Pharisee* that we love to condemn in others.

Healthy, long-term recovery requires that we recognize and admit our responsibility in relationships. We must be willing to admit to ourselves, and at least one other person, how others have been hurt by our selfish actions. Recovery also requires that we seek forgiveness for the harm we have caused to others, and pursue it with a humility that puts others before us. And, *regardless of whether others are willing to reconcile with us or not, we are responsible to forgive others.*

With forgiveness as our hope and pursuit, let us once again work to identify our resentments. When this is a struggle, we admit our struggle to God and to another person. Then, we begin investing ourselves in the lives of others, working to help heal the world around us one person, one situation at a time. As we do this consistently, positive momentum builds inside of us. The way we see ourselves will change. Such positive inner momentum changes the way we relate to others, bringing healthy changes to our families, our communities, our workplaces, and our churches.

It is not just our circumstances that we want improved.

We want to help other people heal, and to see their circumstances improve as well.

BECOMING RELATIONALLY RESPONSE-ABLE

The power to love others begins with the redemptive work of loving and living well with ourselves. Our interior health is a contributor *and* a by-product of our commitment to help others. With this in mind, our work remains simply this: to make a list of the people we have hurt and become willing to make amends to them wherever possible.

In some cases, this will include forgiving others for the wrongs they have done to us. Excuses, procrastination, and delay may be understandable, but they are roadblocks to our recovery if we don't do the work to forgive.

"Therefore, if you are offering your gift at the altar and there remember that your brother or sister has some-

thing against you, leave your gift there in front of the altar. First go and be reconciled to them; then come and offer your gift."

~ *MATTHEW 5:23–24*

THE POISON OF RESENTMENT

While I was working on my *amends list,* I felt strong surges of resentment against a few people who had hurt me terribly when I was a child. I asked God to help me forgive them, but forgiveness was a hard journey. I talked with my sponsor and my counselor about the resentments I felt, and told them exactly why I felt the way I did. These conversations helped me be responsible — *response-able,* once again — for my feelings, which helped me be more forgiving to myself first, and then to others. Today I recognize that while others have harmed me, any resentment I hold against them is a significant cause of my emotional pain.

> *Resentment poisons our hearts. Then it circulates into every part of our lives. It's like taking poison and expecting someone else to get sick and die.*
>
> ~ *VARIATION OF ORIGINAL QUOTE FROM MALACHY MCCOURT*

Once I stopped looking for reasons to be resentful, I was better able to embrace my shortcomings *and* my strengths. I even felt God's strength moving into me through my shortcomings.

The fully felt experience of being forgiven happens organically inside of us as we work to forgive others. This is a work of the mind and body and soul. It helps us see how we have been made with God's providence in mind. As we make a list of those we have hurt, and as we become willing to help them, we become part of the life-renewing goodness that God wants to give to us all.

> *Don't speak evil against each other, dear brothers and sisters. If you criticize and judge each other, then you are criticizing and judging God's law. But your job is to obey the law, not to judge whether it applies to you. God alone, who gave the law, is the Judge. He alone has the power to save or to destroy. So what right do you have to judge your neighbor?*
>
> *~ JAMES 4:11–12 NLT*

However, we must understand that our personality, our talent, and our charm will not be enough to make amends. People need love that is not based on who we are. They need love based on the one who made all of us. Attempts to love others by our own power, no matter how dedicated we may be, often result in various well-meaning but broken forms of codependency. Effectively loving others grows from a connection with real love, which only comes from — you guessed it — God.

NEW DISCOVERIES

As I went about making the list of people who had been harmed by my addictions, it occurred to me how amazing it was that anyone still loved me considering the selfish ways I had sometimes treated them. I realized they didn't love me because I deserved it, they loved me simply because they loved me. This helped me appreciate how loving relationships are precious gifts to be treasured. *We don't need to prove anything to be loved.*

> *Until you conquer the fear of being an outsider, an outsider you will remain.*
>
> ~ C. S. Lewis, The Weight of Glory, *PG. 154*

With guidance from our sponsors and counselors, we set clear boundaries for ourselves, and we respected the boundaries that others set for themselves even when it limited our perceived freedom. To make amends means that we are willing to make them unconditionally, and to make *living amends* by how we live going forward.

There is little value in proclaiming good intentions. The greater value happens when we live our lives in socially responsible ways.

But if we ignore the opportunity to right a wrong, we shut the doors and windows of the spiritual home that God is building inside of us. Darkness closes in, and we miss the leading of God's Spirit. This creates more of the chaos we are working to escape.

As recovering men and women, we work to connect our head to our heart, and our heart to our hands and feet, where we make our amends one person, one situation at a time. With our feet set on the foundation of God's love and care, and within a supportive recovery fellowship, we have everything we need to live response-ably in this world.

By the time I came to recovery, my resentments were so deeply embedded in me that I wasn't aware of the simmering anger inside of me. My internalized anger fueled my self-destructiveness. One day in a counseling session, my counselor had me read something written by someone else who was early in their recovery. By the time I read the third sentence I had broken into tears; it took me several minutes to compose myself. Waiting patiently, my counselor asked me what I was feeling. The only response I could give was that I had been waiting all of my life for the freedom those words expressed.

Later that day I went home and wrote the following:

I survived childhood physical, emotional, and sexual abuse. But now, I no longer consider myself a victim. With God's help, a change has come over me — my attitude is different. I no longer need to destroy myself or others with anger and hate. I don't need to entertain thoughts of revenge. God knows what happened. He knows all the facts. He knows the truth. He will make the correct judgments and punishments as he sees fit, and according to his mercy. He will be just, so I leave them in His hands.

I will not be judged for what happened to me, but I will be judged by how I let it affect my life, and how my life affects others. I am not to blame for what happened to me as a child but I am responsible for my actions, and for what I do with what I know. I cannot change the past, but as God is my strength, I can change my future and I can help others with their future.

I will do my best to take every opportunity to heal. As I heal, the healing in my life will spread throughout future generations.

Personal Reflections

PERSONAL REFLECTIONS

EMBRACING THE WORLD AROUND US

We made direct amends to such people wherever possible, except when to do so would injure them or others.

~ STEP NINE FROM THE TWELVE STEPS

"This is how I want you to conduct yourself in these matters. If you enter your place of worship and, about to make an offering, you suddenly remember a grudge a friend has against you, abandon your offering, leave immediately, go to this friend and make things right. Then and only then, come back and work things out with God."

~ MATTHEW 5:24 MSG

We love each other because he loved us first. If someone says, "I love God," but hates a fellow believer, that person is a liar; for if we don't love people we can see, how can we love God, whom we cannot see? And he has given us this command: Those who love God must also love their fellow believers.

~ 1 JOHN 4:19–21 NLT

"I tell you, love your enemies. Help and give without expecting a return. You'll never—I promise—regret it. Live out this God-created identity the way our Father lives toward us, generously and graciously, even when we're at our worst. Our Father is kind; you be kind."

~ LUKE 6:35–36 MSG

As we said before, it is our responsibility to initiate peace and healing in relationships wherever it is possible. With this in mind, I began to do what I could to help others recover from pain that I had caused them. My sponsor kept reminding me that *helping others was the best way to help myself.* He was quick to tell me that making amends is ego-busting work, and that we may likely face people who deeply resent us.

> *"God blesses those who work for peace, for they will be called the children of God."*
> ~ MATTHEW 5:9 NLT

FACING OUR FEELINGS

For years I held deep resentment against someone who could have stopped the abuse I suffered as a child. For reasons I will never know, he did nothing when he could have protected me. The hurt and anger I felt towards him was buried so deep that I didn't realize I felt the way I did. As I grew older, I repressed my rage more and more, and my addictions increased right along with my hidden hurt and anger. Rage had blinded me so much; I couldn't see the ways I had hurt him. But once in recovery, I couldn't avoid my feelings any longer. I had to face the anger I felt, and with help from others, I did.

Even though his wrongs against me far exceeded anything I had done to him, if I was to heal, I couldn't hold his wrongs against him. I called him on the phone and apologized for my actions. I offered to do whatever I could to heal the hurt I had caused him. His response was a quick and dismissive "I don't want to talk about it."

As many abusers will do, he preferred to keep me at a distance, wanting to keep me hanging by the rope of guilt and obligation.

As heartbreaking as it was, he never acknowledged the abandonment and pain he caused me. Nevertheless, his refusal to acknowledge his betrayal of me didn't stand in the way of my recovery. I forgive him not because he deserves forgiveness, but so that I can move on from the damage he did to me!

In recovery, we learn to be more honest about how things were growing up.

We don't make excuses for our family, or for ourselves.

TRUE FORGIVENESS

True forgiveness cannot be earned or demanded. It does not condone, excuse, or minimize wrongdoing. True forgiveness looks directly at the wrong and the wrongdoer, knowing the full, painful impact of hurtful actions, recognizes the person for who they are, and offers the mercy and grace of a reconnected *but changed* relationship.

People who truly forgive look upon others, even the most disturbed, and see them as someone whom God loves. As we forgive, we honor God by offering appropriate love and respect, no matter how undeserving someone may be. This does not mean that our relationships will be as they were before. We may never have the same freedom we had before. We may never have the complete, unmitigated trust we had in the past.

Damaged relationships should change, with healthier boundaries set in place.

Improved boundaries are a beneficial consequence of the hurt-healing process.

It is not until we love a person in all his ugliness that we can make him beautiful, or ourselves either.

~ *Frederick Buechner,* The Magnificent Defeat, *pg. 42*

When I struggled to forgive someone, I prayed for them. I found that praying for them helped me move beyond the resentment that blocked my growth. I prayed for them in the same way I prayed for myself: that God would give them hope for their life, grace for their struggles, help with their difficulties, and courage to live abundantly. As I prayed in this way, I realized that any assumptions I had about others forgiving me made the forgiveness I might receive feel coerced and insincere.

Assumption and entitlement reduce forgiveness to shallow appeasement. I'm sure you will agree that feeling appeased is not something we need.

You were cleansed from your sins when you obeyed the truth, so now you must show sincere love to each other as brothers and sisters. Love each other deeply with all your heart.

~ *1 Peter 1:22 NLT*

Put yourself aside, and help others get ahead. Don't be obsessed with getting your own advantage. Forget yourselves long enough to lend a helping hand.

~ *Philippians 2:3 MSG*

As others set their boundaries, we should also set our boundaries. When someone has done something inexcusable to us, we should recognize it for the inexcusable act it was. For best insight, we should discuss these issues with our sponsor and our counselor. Their guidance will give us insight regarding how we can be healthy and balanced going forward.

For our part, let's not ask for forgiveness when we are really asking to be excused for our wrongdoing. Even when unintentional, wrongdoing is not an accident. Accidents can be excused, but people who do selfish, wrong things need forgiveness. Sincerely asking for forgiveness is an act of repentance. Repentance does not debate or bargain, nor does it rationalize or make excuses.

ACTIONS SPEAK LOUDER THAN WORDS

I did my level best to approach those I had hurt with humility and gentleness. I considered it my response-ability to give them back the dignity I had taken. I acknowledged that they never deserved to be treated the way I treated them — that, in fact, they deserved much better. The message I had for them was very simple: *Today I see things differently than I did in the past. I am less important; God and other people are more important.*

There were times when it felt like other people were out to get me. When I was open to learn, I realized that the attacks I felt were directed at my addictive thinking, my selfish actions, and the sinfully distorted way I had treated others. Today, I do my best not to defend myself when I feel attacked. If I have done something wrong, triggering an aggressive response from someone else, I apologize for what I did wrong and ask what I can do to make things right.

Our actions speak louder than our words.

This is the kind of life you've been invited into, the kind of life Christ lived. He suffered everything that came his way so you would know that it could be done, and also know how to do it, step-by-step.

> *He never did one thing wrong, Not once said anything amiss. They called him every name in the book and he said nothing back.*
>
> ~ 1 Peter 2:21–23 MSG

> *The people who gave you the consequences are not your enemies. By seeing those who give you consequences as the enemy, you keep yourself stuck in justifying your behavior. Your real problem is your denial and self-delusion.*
>
> ~ Patrick Carnes, PhD, Facing the Shadow, pg. 16

In the process of doing our work, we learned that making *amends to ourselves* created *spiritual momentum* in our healing, which helped us make amends to others. This is because our inner health is an essential ingredient in our relationships, second only to God's loving presence in importance. Some may disagree with this, but no one suffers from sexual addiction more than the one who is sexually addicted. To have healthier relationships with others requires that we build a healthier relationship with ourselves.

Many of us needed to make changes in our eating and exercise habits. When we had hurt ourselves financially, we faced it and made changes to build financial stability. When we had hurt ourselves emotionally through self-pity and by blaming others, we faced the abusive nature of self-pity and how we had made ourselves out to be a victim. We discussed all of this with our sponsors and counselors.

Sometimes we wrote ourselves amends letters, addressing them to ourselves at specific ages from our childhood, our teenage years, even our years as an adult. We sat in front of a mirror, and read these letters to ourselves, face-to-face. We also read these letters to our sponsors, and to our counselors, and to some of our recovery partners. Most of all, we gave ourselves grace and understanding, and made peace with the reality of our ups and downs.

Recovery is not a straight line from beginning to end.

No matter how good or how bad things get, one thing is for sure: things are going to change.

EXPERIENCING THE FREE LIFE

Our work of making amends helps us learn to love ourselves more like God loves us. It is about far more than just being free from our addictions. It is being free to live across the broad scope of our day-to-day experience. We don't ever "possess" this freedom, but it never leaves us either. It is a natural by-product of knowing God's forgiveness personally, and knowing with assurance that he will never take it back. Yes, we can turn our backs on God, but when we are ready to reach out for him, he will be close at hand and ready to help.

> *It is not possible to love others unless our hearts are growing in faith and hope. Faith and hope birth love as we live out our calling in anticipation of his coming.*
>
> *~ DAN B. ALLENDER, THE HEALING PATH, PG. 164*

Because of the many problems that our addictions created in our relationships, we consulted with our sponsors and counselors about how to speak with our loved ones in the most caring way. We had to speak honestly, yet without hurting them even more by sharing unnecessary details. We learned that sharing in a general way opens the door for communication. Most importantly, it opened the door for them to share their honest thoughts and feelings with us.

In situations where we faced serious consequences or the possibility of strong temptations, we again asked our sponsors and counselors for guidance.

Some amends should never be made face-to-face.

We will be of little help to anyone if, to clear our own conscience, we walk ourselves into overwhelming temptation. We must stay safe from any situation where we might lose the recovery we have already gained, and old partners, with no ill will, might possibly derail our recovery. Our sponsors and counselors helped us know how to handle each situation. If God wants us to see former lovers, he will arrange it in a way where we can be safe.

A Word of Caution

While it may not be wise to contact old partners directly, we can make amends virtually by helping people who represent our old partners in some way. For example, changing our attitude toward sexually attractive people in general, and respecting the dignity of all people, is a wonderful beginning. Also, letting go of our memories of sexual conquest, or our fantasies of make-believe romance, is a great way to move forward in the healing process. When we no longer see others as objects for pleasure and reward, and by retraining our minds by praying for those we have held hostage in our memories and fantasies, the negative power of our memories and fantasies will begin to lose its grip on us.

Perhaps the best place to start is by praying for old acquaintances and lovers. Pray for their health, their safety, and their happiness. Pray that they would experience the fulfillment of their God-shaped hopes and dreams. As we do this consistently, we will develop a strong, wholesome resilience against the powerful, spontaneous stimulations that once drove us to do things we would later regret.

As we acknowledge the God-given dignity inside of all people and pray for their well-being, we will see past what is sometimes an overwhelming distraction of physical beauty, seeing them completely, as God sees them.

We don't need to "have" anyone. We can simply enjoy them as friends who are free to come and go.

PERSONAL REFLECTIONS

PERSONAL REFLECTIONS

INTEGRITY

We continued to take personal inventory and when we were wrong, promptly admitted it.

~ STEP TEN FROM THE TWELVE STEPS

You could fall flat on your face as easily as anyone else. Forget about self-confidence; it's useless. Cultivate God-confidence.

~ 1 CORINTHIANS 10:12 MSG

How can I know all the sins lurking in my heart? Cleanse me from these hidden faults.

~ PSALM 19:12 NLT

We justify our actions by appearances; GOD examines our motives.

~ PROVERBS 21:2 MSG

In our soul-searching process, many of us came to see how we had been overly concerned with being attractive or impressing others. We had been more concerned with *looking* good than with simply *being* a good person. Our obsession to impress reflected our feelings of inadequacy. Our obsessive self-doubt stood against the freedom our hearts longed to know. As we continue to go further in recovery, we must take a risk and be true to ourselves no matter what people may think or say.

Integrity is impossible without authenticity.

To continue growing, we must continue to pursue a healthy awareness of our motives, and the hidden thoughts and feelings behind them. We must acknowledge our warped self-perceptions and accept who we are, which means preferring God's design for our life above our own.

Consistent growth requires that we never forget that we are powerless over our sexual addiction, and that our lives are beyond our ability to manage on our own. And let's never forget that when our life seemed most hopeless, we saw how other people were recovering from their addictions, and we came to believe that we could recover right along with them. We then made the decision to trust God with our lives, recognizing that our relationship with him had to grow as he guided the process. Along the way, we learned that our recovery was a gift from God *and* a responsibility that we needed to care for.

We began admitting to ourselves, to God, and to a few well-chosen people who and what we were inside and out. As we honestly shared ourselves with others, we found ourselves dissatisfied with the way we had masqueraded through life. We knew we needed God's help to change our character flaws, and so we asked him to make changes in our character according to his design. Over time, our spiritual eyes opened wider and our character flaws weakened, which helped us take responsibility for how we had hurt people around us. We now do our best to reconcile with others, starting with forgiving those who have hurt us, and helping those who have been hurt by our addictions. This recovery plan has taken us on a journey, but we can't stop now. What benefit would we gain, what usefulness could we offer, if we abandoned our journey incomplete?

*I don't mean to say that I have already achieved these
things or that I have already reached perfection. But I
press on to possess that perfection for which Christ Jesus
first possessed me. No, dear brothers and sisters, I have
not achieved it, but I focus on this one thing: Forgetting
the past and looking forward to what lies ahead, I press
on to reach the end of the race and receive the heavenly
prize for which God, through Christ Jesus, is calling us.*

~ *PHILIPPIANS 3:12–14 NLT*

PRACTICE MAKES PROGRESS

My recovery partners and I practice these Twelve Step principles
every day. They help me keep an honest view of myself and my
motives. God doesn't tell me to bring my failures to him just
once. He encourages me to bring my failures to him day in and
day out.

*So let's not allow ourselves to get fatigued doing good. At
the right time we will harvest a good crop if we don't give
up, or quit. Right now, therefore, every time we get the
chance, let us work for the benefit of all, starting with
the people closest to us in the community of faith.*

~ *GALATIANS 6:9 MSG*

*GOD is in charge of human life, watching and examin-
ing us inside and out.*

~ *PROVERBS 20:27 MSG*

As was said before, recovery is an ongoing process of healing and character development. When we realize that we lack character, we admit it. When we admit a shortfall in our character, we are actively working to improve it. And yet improvement in our character is more a gift from God than something we create on our own. Every time we admit our wrongdoing and sincerely work to correct our mistakes, we live more deeply within the spiritual framework of God's loving character.

> *If the Spirit of God detects anything in you that is wrong, He does not ask you to put it right; He asks you to accept the light, and He will put it right. A child of the light confesses instantly and stands bared before God; a child of the darkness says — "Oh, I can explain that away." When once the light breaks and the conviction of wrong comes, be a child of the light, and confess, and God will deal with what is wrong; if you vindicate yourself, you prove yourself to be a child of the darkness.*
>
> ~ OSWALD CHAMBERS, MY UTMOST FOR HIS HIGHEST, *MARCH 23 ENTRY*

> *What helps at this point is to see your consequences as your teachers. You have been sent a lesson to learn. If you don't learn the lesson this time, it will manifest itself again, and probably in a more painful form the next time.*
>
> ~ PATRICK CARNES, PhD, FACING THE SHADOW, *PG. 17*

Together with our recovery partners, let's do our best to guard against pride and overconfidence. Everything finds its right place and value when we do our work honestly. Even from the discouragement of failure, stronger motivation for more healing forms inside of us.

This changes everything!

The power to honor the truth — to speak it and be it — is at the heart of true masculinity.

~ *LEANNE PAYNE,* CRISIS IN MASCULINITY, *PG. 41*

PERSONAL REFLECTIONS

PERSONAL REFLECTIONS

LISTEN INTENTLY, SPEAK SOFTLY, LIVE POWERFULLY

Sought through prayer and meditation to improve our conscious contact with God as we understood Him, praying only for the knowledge of His will for us and the power to carry that out.

~ STEP ELEVEN FROM THE TWELVE STEPS

Let petitions and praises shape your worries into prayers, letting God know your concerns. Before you know it, a sense of God's wholeness, everything coming together for good, will come and settle you down. It's wonderful what happens when Christ displaces worry at the center of your life.

~ PHILIPPIANS 4:6–7 MSG

"Here's what I want you to do: Find a quiet, secluded place so you won't be tempted to role-play before God. Just be there as simply and honestly as you can manage. The focus will shift from you to God, and you will begin to sense his grace."

~ MATTHEW 6:6 MSG

Be still in the presence of the LORD, and wait patiently for him to act. Don't worry about evil people who prosper or fret about their wicked schemes.

~ PSALM 37:7 NLT

I have never had a better life than the one I have today. It is a happy, healthy life, like the one I needed when I was a child. I will never forget those early formative years; I felt so isolated and lost to self-loathing. But today, my view of those years has changed. Redemption has molded hardship into something good. I breath in eternal grace and exhale resilient joy because of what God has given to me as I have worked the recovery process.

And yet, even as full as I feel, a restless longing still lives inside of me. It's as if I've walked a thousand miles longing for home and the last mile is a steep uphill climb. The restless longing I still feel compels me forward on the journey.

I know I am not alone with this.

The deep, hidden current of every destructive behavior is a longing that exists unheard and unsatisfied because no earthly thing can satisfy the longing of our God-created human soul.

We have this longing from birth. It is a natural, eternal desire.

Every man or woman who has come to our fellowship will freely admit that their best efforts brought only temporary relief and gratification. As they got honest and admitted their need, and the reality of their failed efforts, their restless longing began to be transformed. The process of their recovery work guided them deeper into God's grace, where their restlessness was reshaped into a soul-engaging energy that compelled them even deeper into healing.

We make the decision to surrender our lives to God, not because we are good or honorable, or even because we want to. *No one gets to know God because of their good intentions or virtue.* We surrender our lives to save ourselves from the inner turmoil that we cannot escape on our own, and that is when we come face-to-face with our lifesaving God!

God's love is found when we seek him with the urgent longing of our restless soul.

We have all had our own personal reasons for why we surrendered our lives to God's care. Some of them sounded good, while others sounded rather selfish. Whatever our reasons, they were more than good enough because there is not a bad reason to recover from the broken condition of our lives. *Over time, our souls found more depth and honesty, and we sought God for the best reason of all: God himself.*

SOUL YEARNINGS

The work of recovery teaches us to be circumspect about why our souls are not yet fully satisfied, and yet they are fulfilled. There is more paradox here. Paradox exists in our core: the phenomenon of our God-created spirituality that lives side-by-side with our natural bent toward addicted self-destruction, both of which motivate us to find God.

Spirituality — perhaps best thought of as simplicity — is experienced as we live the life God offers to us, one day at a time, without demanding that it be any more than what it is.

Personal fulfillment comes in the process, not from the end goal.

Our addicted soul, with its compulsive neediness, comes to understand that with God there is always enough. *Faith is not only a belief system; it is God-centered belonging that leads to healthy living.* We learn to have our satisfaction in our simple, daily work and life, where rest is not a reward as much as it is preparation for the next leg of our journey.

It is simply like this: with God, life has infinite possibilities for good; without God, enduring goodness is impossible to hold on to. This simple understanding will transform everything we think and do. As we remember this, we will live privately in the same way we would if the eyes of the whole world were on us.

We must live our lives before God, knowing that He sees all and that our reward will come from Him if we persist in doing what He has asked us to do.

~ *Joyce Meyer*

Our sponsors and counselors will always be valuable resources. Some of us also sought out *spiritual directors* for more in-depth spiritual guidance. Spiritual directors are people trained to lead others in spiritual disciplines that date back centuries, but are not commonly practiced in modern, Western religious cultures. All of these wonderful people, our sponsors, counselors, and our spiritual directors, played important roles in our growth, but they were never our source for healing and change. Our *one-and-only, new-person-Christ life* grows more from the influence of God's Spirit working deep within us than from the good influences of others.

No Accidents in Recovery

We increase our suffering when we withhold ourselves from a total, willing surrender to God. And yet, we hold ourselves back more often than we know. Once again, this is the subtle, destructive, and I will even add, *almost imperceptible* nature of denial.

Denial makes us think we are stronger than our failures indicate.

Here is something important to remember: the bigger our ego gets, the smaller our view of God gets. However, when we pursue God's presence in earnest, God's loving power takes over and our ego shrinks. We will always be imperfect in this world, but in the eyes of God we are already spiritually complete, even as we work to grow in our surrender.

This is why there are no accidents in recovery.

One miracle of recovery is the new life story that grows from our recovery experience. The story of our life will become an encouragement to others just as others have inspired us in recovery. Healthy, balanced, recovering people are an example of how God takes the broken pieces of human experience and creates something beautiful for the world to behold.

> *We take our efforts seriously, while knowing that serious results are from God. We remain intent and dogged in pursuit of our disciplines, in the working of the steps, but dismiss at all times the notion that our work is enough. It never is. Our miracles come from God, and He offers them in conjunction with our work.*
>
> ~ *Oswald Chambers,* My Utmost for His Highest, *February 9 entry*

Much of what we realized in our Step Four work, and admitted in Step Five, showed just how unfaithful and alone we had felt in the past. We were like adulterous lovers who had been found out. By doing our recovery work, we are returning home, often awkward and embarrassed and ashamed, sneaking in the back door, not knowing exactly what to say. To our surprise, God has been waiting for us with open arms. He has already made the first move to attend to our needs. Let us be willing to make the second move, which is to pray.

The anguished groans that resonate from our deepest shame will perhaps become our most beautiful prayer. It is the beautifully human way that we break through our silence. It is the brave cry of our need to know, and our passionate desire to be known.

> *Prayer is man's impulse to open up his life at its deepest level. People pray because they cannot help it. In one way or another, I think, all people pray.*
>
> ~ *Frederick Buechner*, The Magnificent Defeat, *pg. 126*

Prayer puts us at the kitchen table, with coffee mug in hand, ready for a face-to-face encounter, and an increased bond of connection and friendship with God. It ushers us into communion with the perfect spiritual Father. While God is perfect, our prayers don't ever need to be. What we find impossible to express, he understands. What we don't know how to say, God's Spirit will say for us. *The simplicity of honest prayer catapults us into the wild frontier of an authentic spiritual life.*

> *In prayer, real prayer, we begin to think God's thoughts after Him: to desire the things He desires, to love the things He loves, to will the things He wills. Progressively, we are taught to see things from His point of view.*
>
> ~ *Richard J. Foster*, Celebration of Discipline, *pg. 34*

To escape from my addictions and my self-centeredness, I had to become a man who prays. It is always the most relevant thing that I do. Prayer helps me see the connection between the self-created catastrophe of my past and the God-designed providence of my future. Prayer helps me know who I am and what I should do at any moment in time. In prayer, I find the alertness to live well in difficult moments, and prayer gives me the tenacity to meet overwhelming challenges. Prayer helps me work with God to determine what kind of man I will be, how my future will be made, and what impact my life will make on the world.

It is sometimes helpful to pray for others to change. It is always helpful to pray that I will change. As prayer changes me, prayer changes the influence I have on my surroundings. Then, through the lens of this *prayer-full* perspective, the world around me is changed in a better way than I could ever change it.

> *"Keep on asking, and you will receive what you ask for. Keep on seeking, and you will find. Keep on knocking, and the door will be opened to you. For everyone who asks, receives. Everyone who seeks, finds. And to everyone who knocks, the door will be opened."*
>
> *~ Matthew 7:7–8 NLT*

A Different Kind of Work

Just like any other good relationship, our relationship with God is interactive. Meditation is our *listening* role as we interact with God. It is a discipline, and a way of life that enables us to hear his voice, discern his guidance, and accept the life-giving power he wants to bless us with.

As we well know, recovery is hard work, but meditation is a different kind of work. It is not about effort; it is about quieting our mind, body, and spirit so we can hear and perceive what we need to know. Oftentimes, the best thing we can do to grow our spiritual life is to stop.

Stop working. Stop playing. Stop everything.

Be still. Be quiet. Listen.

In contemporary society our Adversary majors in three things: noise, hurry, and crowds. If he (the enemy) can keep us engaged in "muchness" and "manyness," he will rest satisfied.

~ Richard J. Foster, Celebration of Discipline, *pg. 15*

Hurry is not of the Devil, it is the Devil.

~ Carl Jung

In meditation, we set our distractions aside the best we can to make time and space for God. We intentionally make the time, go to a place, and mentally make space for his presence to abide. We wait there, and listen for the spiritual sound of his voice. As we do this, we will see him reorganize our concerns and priorities in ways that are healthy and useful. Our unseen agendas and motivations get reworked supernaturally. God doesn't speak to us because of our special abilities. He speaks to us when we are naked and honest before him, desiring to hear from him and open to following his guidance.

Meditation is a bit of a spiritual art form but it requires no particular skill; anyone can do it, and do it beautifully. Like anything else, we learn to meditate by simply starting. We start, get distracted, start again, get distracted, and then start again. Over time, and with every renewed start, we become better at hearing and listening to the voice of God, and discerning his will. Absolutely nothing is lost in this process because meditation does not empty or detach us from what is important. Meditation actually results in a filling and reattachment of our heart and mind to God's heart and mind.

Meditation deepens our friendship with Jesus.

It deepens our spiritual confidence that God will speak to us personally, that he will act on our behalf, and that he will guide us to healthy, courageous action.

Because most of us have never done it, meditation may feel uncomfortable and perhaps intimidating. It was for me at first. Let's not put pressure on ourselves. Meditation is not a test or a competition. We don't have to do it *well* for it to be fruitful. We just have to do it.

One aspect of meditation is letting your imagination run freely, like a child's imagination will do. After all, God put imagination inside of us for a good purpose — that was true when we were children, and it is true now. Our addictions reduced our capacity for imagination and creative thinking, but as we meditate, our minds heal and reopen to the wonderful world of possibilities and goal setting that God has built into us. We should often think about the many possible ways that God can reveal himself to us, change us, restore us, and use us. But remember this: God has no obligation to fulfill selfish ideas we dream up. We must not allow "meditation" to devolve into self-centeredness, which is most dangerous when it is hidden in self-centered, pretty-faced, religious pretending.

If we are interested in walking with God, we must prefer faithfulness and obedience over comfort and blessing. The disciplines of prayer and meditation will teach us to listen quietly, speak softly, and live powerfully.

"Are you seeking great things for yourself? Don't do it!"

~ Jeremiah 45:5 NLT

Yet you don't have what you want because you don't ask God for it. And even when you ask, you don't get it because your motives are all wrong—you want only what will give you pleasure.

~ James 4:2–3 NLT

PERSONAL REFLECTIONS

PERSONAL REFLECTIONS

DESTINY ARRIVES AND WE SHOW UP

Having had a spiritual awakening as the result of these Steps, we tried to carry the message to others, and to practice these principles in all our affairs.

~ Step Twelve from the Twelve Steps

Live creatively, friends. If someone falls into sin, forgivingly restore him, saving your critical comments for yourself. You might be needing forgiveness before the day's out. Stoop down and reach out to those who are oppressed. Share their burdens, and so complete Christ's law. If you think you are too good for that, you are badly deceived.

~ Galatians 6:1–3 MSG

Then he turned to the host. "The next time you put on a dinner, don't just invite your friends and family and rich neighbors, the kind of people who will return the favor. Invite some people who never get invited out, the misfits from the wrong side of the tracks. You'll be—and experience—a blessing. They won't be able to return the favor, but the favor will be returned—oh, how it will be returned!—at the resurrection of God's people."

~ Luke 14:12–14 MSG

Embracing what God does for you is the best thing you can do for him. Don't become so well-adjusted to your culture that you fit into it without even thinking. Instead, fix your attention on God. You'll be changed from the inside out. Readily recognize what he wants from you, and quickly respond to it. Unlike the culture around you, always dragging you down to its level of immaturity, God brings the best out of you, develops well-formed maturity in you.

~ *ROMANS 12:1–2 MSG*

I never wanted to become a sex addict. I certainly never imagined that it would take hold of my life the way it did. As a matter of fact, getting addicted to anything was the furthest thing from my mind. Once I realized how serious my problem was, all I wanted was to recover from my addictions, because of their horribly destructive consequences.

However, through the ongoing work of recovery I have received more healing and goodness than I ever thought I needed. It takes time to understand this, but the work of recovery is about so much more than just survival. The healing of my addictions continues to be an astounding personal journey, full of twists and turns, leading me ever deeper into radical personal transformation. I have changed, and I continue to change, gaining more wisdom and insight than I could ever get from a book, in a classroom or office, or from another person.

I once thought of myself as a physical person who was trying to have spiritual experiences. Now I think of myself as a spiritual person who experiences life in ways God personally designed for me. I am a man who has been sexually addicted, but now, having offered myself to God, I consider myself the most blessed of all men.

A NEW PURPOSE

As we continue our work in recovery, gratitude for our addictions will grow. This may sound incredible, but I have actually come to think of my addictions as important preparation. I often call them *pre-recovery preparation.*

My addictions, after being healed by God's grace through the work of recovery, have made me someone who embodies the prodigal experience of selfishness, disaster, despair, desperate cries for help, discovery of God's gracious power to change, and a life resurrected and renewed.

Is there is a better plan for any of us?

Today, having spent every resource of my own, my purpose is to seek, discover, and experience God as Jesus Christ knows God. As God's power comes alive inside of me, I encourage others to seek, discover, and experience God for themselves.

Aren't we all prodigals in one way or another? (See Luke 15:11–32 for Jesus' story of the prodigal.)

> *Listen to your life. See it for the fathomless mystery that it is. In the boredom and pain of it no less than in the excitement and gladness: touch, taste, smell your way to the holy and hidden heart of it because in the last analysis all moments are key moments, and life itself is grace.*
>
> ~ *FREDERICK BUECHNER*, NOW AND THEN, *PG. 87*

I am proud of my growth and the growth of those who share recovery with me. We are well prepared to do serious business with God, and with other people. We have seen for ourselves how God has a future uniquely designed for each and all of his children. As we follow his plan individually, and collectively as a fellowship, we are well equipped to offer goodness to anyone we may encounter.

I consider myself a *recovering* — or as some will prefer, *recovered* — sex addict. I admit that my brain makes a spontaneous wrong turn every now and then, creating a conflict of impulse and desire inside of me. Yes, I respect the dangerous nature of temptation, but I do not fear it, because I've learned that it's not an inescapable calamity.

Temptation reminds us there are risks in life and that we must be diligent in our recovery.

The thing that most ensures our ongoing recovery is the maintenance of our spiritual surrender to God. He alone has the power to keep us safe from our impulsive, selfish nature. The temptations we experience are uncomfortable sometimes, and at other times they can be miserable. When we feel conflicted, let's be quick to admit that we are powerless over our addictions, and that our life is unmanageable by our own strength, and yet by following the way of Jesus, we will continue to recover and live a better life.

Each time we feel the urge to chase after our old, addicted way of life but don't, the obsessions of addiction lose some of their power. New attachments for goodness are created inside of us with each obedient decision, ultimately gaining strength over the old destructive mindset that played into our addictions. Even better yet, we will lose selfish interest in our own life as we become more interested in sharing God's redeeming life with others.

POSSESSED BY GOD

God's gift of new life is not without a personal cost. We claim it only by living with surrendered cooperation. God gives us everything we need, which is why we give our lives back to him in the way we live them out. This builds the gift of gratitude, which further nourishes our God-designed desires, making *every* area of our life an act of surrender and worship.

> *For He claims all, because He is love and must bless. He cannot bless us unless He has us. When we try to keep within us an area that is our own, we try to keep an area of death. Therefore, in love, He claims all. There's no bargaining with Him.*
>
> ~ *C. S. LEWIS,* THE WEIGHT OF GLORY, *PG. 190*

> *This inrush of God's Holy Spirit heals us naturally — naturally. But it does far more than that. Indeed, as we pursue the spiritual life we lose sight of the physical benefits in our increasing vision of God Himself. We find after a while that we desire God more for His own sake than for ours.*
>
> ~ *AGNES SANFORD,* THE HEALING LIGHT, *PG. 60*

> *"You can't keep it unless you give it away."*
>
> ~ *A COMMON SAYING IN ALCOHOLICS ANONYMOUS*

What started with Bill Wilson and Dr. Bob Smith, two alcoholics helping each other stay sober, has resulted in a movement that continues to help millions of men and women recover from alcoholism and drug addiction. AA also spawned the Al-

Anon movement, which helps millions of individuals and families who have been hurt by their loved ones' drinking and/or drug use. Just like Bill Wilson and Dr. Smith, in recovery we become a gift to each other and to the world — one moment, one situation, one person at a time.

The greatest needs of our day will not be met by counselors, doctors, or professionals. They will be met by recovering people like you and me.

We are grateful leaders in pain suffered, and humble servants in recovery gained. We are men and women who have joined the holy fight for our own lives, and for the lives of others. The great need in our world remains the same today as it has always been: godly women and men who display a quality of character that ignites a desire in others to know God in a way that changes them from the inside out.

No one can live our role better than we can. We call out to anyone who is dead and dying in his or her struggles, problems, addictions, and sins. We say to them, "Come with us, we are going to God. We are going to Life."

> *Those of us who are strong and able in the faith need to step in and lend a hand to those who falter, and not just do what is most convenient for us. Strength is for service, not status. Each one of us needs to look after the good of the people around us, asking ourselves, "How can I help?"*
>
> *~ ROMANS 15:1 MSG*

> *We want to live well, but our foremost efforts should be to help others live well.*
>
> *~ 1 CORINTHIANS 10:24 MSG*

IT'S NOT ABOUT US

If we think our recovery and healing is ours alone, we have neither recovered nor have we experienced true healing. When we believe our recovery is to be lived to helps others, our lives will prove that we are healing already. We face eternal choices day in and day out, with every breath we take.

Who owns you, who will you live for?

Will you live for God and others, or suffer in your addiction and shame?

But serving others is not the end, it is just a new beginning. All too easily, we compartmentalize our lives, gaining ground in some ways and losing ground in others, when it is our life as a whole that matters most. Carrying a hope-filled message to others helps ensure our continuing growth in sexual integrity. We must be willing to do all that we can, one day at a time, to ensure that we are cleansed and healed deeply, so when someone comes to us in need and looking for answers to their questions, we will be ready to guide them into their own experience with Jesus and recovery.

FINAL QUESTIONS

My experience in recovery has changed the way I spend my time, my talents, and my money, as well as changed the foods I eat and the way I conduct my career. Perhaps my recovery is best reflected in the positive changes in my relationships. I have become, and I continue to become, the most blessed of all men. Yet there is still more work to do.

We must continue moving forward, ready and willing to face tough questions so that we can gain a fuller relationship with God and the empowered life that only he can give.

Here are some of the questions we keep coming back to:

- What is it that I am powerless over?

- How is my life unmanageable?

- To whom will I admit my secrets?

- What action step must I take next?

- What are the tough questions that you need to ask yourself?

Before, you and I were afraid to face these kinds of questions and the answers they might reveal. But now we know that hard questions are a lifesaving blessing, and God gives us the ever-conquering courage to face them and answer them with integrity.

Isn't that what we were looking for all along?

PERSONAL REFLECTIONS

PERSONAL REFLECTIONS

MORE BOOKS BY DAVID ZAILER

Our Journey Home

Insights and Inspirations for Christian 12-Step Recovery

Starting Point for Recovery

A Simple 12-Step Guide for Use in Counseling

for Addiction Recovery

Death of a Fisherman

A Memoir of Family, Faith, and Forgiveness

www.ingramcontent.com/pod-product-compliance
Lightning Source LLC
Chambersburg PA
CBHW070706130626
46553CB00005B/1860